Alistair McDowall
Plays: 1

Brilliant Adventures, Captain Amazing, Talk Show, Pomona

Brilliant Adventures: 'Alistair McDowall's fascinating debut plays by its own rules.' *The Times*

Captain Amazing: 'This is a terrific piece of writing – full of crackle, invention and heart.' *The Guardian*

Talk Show: 'The play's energy seems effortless, with subtext swimming in and out of view. The humour, often very funny, oozes desperation . . . In the end, the play . . . asks one simple question: why is it so difficult for people to draw strength from each other?' *The Other Bridge Project*

Pomona: 'Alistair McDowall's slippery, gripping dystopian thriller . . . enthralling, unexpectedly funny and expertly maintained. . . . Clever, creepy and compelling.' *Financial Times*

Alistair McDowall grew up in the north east of England. *Brilliant Adventures* was awarded a Bruntwood Prize in 2011. Other plays include *Talk Show* (Royal Court), *Captain Amazing* (Live Theatre) and *Pomona* (Royal Welsh College/Orange Tree Theatre/National Theatre/Royal Exchange). His work has been translated and produced internationally.

ALISTAIR McDOWALL

Plays: 1

Brilliant Adventures
Captain Amazing
Talk Show
Pomona

*with an introduction by the author
and
foreword by Simon Stephens*

Bloomsbury Methuen Drama
An imprint of Bloomsbury Publishing Plc

BLOOMSBURY

LONDON · OXFORD · NEW YORK · NEW DELHI · SYDNEY

Bloomsbury Methuen Drama
An imprint of Bloomsbury Publishing Plc

50 Bedford Square
London
WC1B 3DP
UK

1385 Broadway
New York
NY 10018
USA

www.bloomsbury.com

Bloomsbury is a registered trade mark of Bloomsbury Publishing Plc

This collection first published 2016

Brilliant Adventures first published in 2013 by Methuen Drama
© Alistair McDowall 2013, 2016

Captain Amazing first published in 2014 by Methuen Drama
© Alistair McDowall 2014, 2016
Illustrations © Rebecca Glover 2014

Talk Show first published in this collection 2016
© Alistair McDowall 2016

Pomona first published in 2014 by Methuen Drama
© Alistair McDowall 2014, 2016

This collection copyright © Alistair McDowall 2016
Introduction copyright © Alistair McDowall 2016
Foreword copyright © Simon Stephens 2016

British Library Cataloguing-in-Publication Data
A catalogue record for this book is available from the British Library.

ISBN: HB: 978-1-3500-0743-7
PB: 978-1-3500-0742-07
ePDF: 978-1-3500-0744-4
ePub: 978-1-3500-0745-1

Library of Congress Cataloging-in-Publication Data
A catalog record for this book is available from the Library of Congress.

Cover design: Adriana Brioso
Cover images: courtesy Luka Hardes; Stu Kiesow; Peter Moore

Typeset by Country Setting, Kingsdown, Kent CT14 8ES

Contents

Alistair McDowall
Select Chronology

2011   *Brilliant Adventures* awarded a Bruntwood Prize for Playwriting.

2012   *Brilliant Adventures* part of the Royal Court Theatre's Young Writers Festival 2012.

2013   *Brilliant Adventures* premieres at the Royal Exchange, Manchester, before transferring to Live Theatre, Newcastle, in a co-production between the Royal Exchange and Live Theatre.

        Talk Show opens at Royal Court Theatre, in the Jerwood Downstairs space, as part of the Open Court season.

        Captain Amazing opens at Live Theatre.

2014   *Pomona* is commissioned and performed by the Royal Welsh College of Music and Drama, in collaboration with the Royal Court.

        Pomona subsequently produced at the Orange Tree Theatre, London.

2015   *Pomona* transfers to the National Theatre's Temporary Theatre, and then to the Royal Exchange.

2016   *X* premieres at the Royal Court Theatre, in the Jerwood Downstairs space, directed by Artistic Director Vicky Featherstone.

Foreword

I have only a handful of ideas about playwriting. I know only about three jokes about theatre. Whenever I'm teaching, I tend to repeat these ideas and these jokes. If you are unfortunate enough to encounter my teaching on more than one occasion, you will notice that I fundamentally repeat the same things time and time again. Sometimes I'm more skilled at hiding this than others.

One of the jokes is based on one of the ideas. I have noticed over the years that playwrights tend to be mutually supportive of one another. Actors pretend to support one another, but secretly are defined by their envy. Directors are openly hostile to one another. Playwrights support one another and that support feels genuine.

Perhaps this is because, on the whole, playwrights have little or no power in theatre, so envy is pointless. Partly it's because, while many actors could play the same role and many directors could direct the same piece, there is no way that playwrights could ever write one another's plays. In British theatre, playwrights tend to be the primary artist, rather than the secondary artist. We generate material, rather than delivering material other people have generated. This generation is a unique consequence of our lives and cultures and experiences. We can't copy one another's lives so there is little point envying one another's work.

Of late, I have started to realise, too, that our plays are not only distinct from one another in this way, but they are also dependent on one another. We make one another better. We steal with fearlessness and spar with one another. We stand on one another's shoulders as we try to imagine our nights in the theatre. We stand on the shoulders – not only of every playwright that has come before us – but on those who come after us.

This mutual dependency leads to a natural affinity, rather than envy. We are doing the same dispiriting, exciting, bewildering job as one another, so we may as well look after one another. In Britain, a country almost uniquely rich in new plays, this dependency – deep and complex – is one I cherish.

I love reading new plays by new writers.

I read about eight hundred new plays when I was the Writers' Tutor at the Royal Court between 2001 and 2006. I've continued reading new writers in my capacity as Associate Playwright at both the Lyric Hammersmith and the Royal Court. I love reading new plays by new writers because the process galvanises me, challenges me to be sharper. My motives are entirely selfish. Reading new plays by new writers makes me a better playwright myself.

No new playwright has excited me or galvanized me, inspired me or touched me, in the time I have been doing this work, with quite the force of Alistair McDowall. No other playwright has made me want to try to be better to quite this extent.

I met him briefly at the end of 2009 and read two of his early plays at the end of 2010 when he sent them to me in my position as Associate at the Lyric. The talent in the plays – one a collection of monologues, the other a brutal study of a girls' boarding school – was undeniable. Already then a recent graduate from Manchester University, Ali wrote with nuance and suppleness. He had a serious engagement with characters attempting to survive with compassion in a world of brutality. He located the essence of this brutality fearlessly in economics. While, on occasion, his early plots felt expositional or inert, the force of his work was raw and undeniable.

I met him on the occasions he would come down to London and read his next play *Jennifer Jane*.

Two things struck me in our correspondence about this early writing. I remember Ali corrected me when I got the title, *Jennifer Jane*, wrong. I had made the title the subject heading of an email to him and erroneously called it *Jennifer James*. Quietly, without drawing attention to it, he corrected my error in his reply. Plays are important things. It matters that we get the titles right. The second thing I noticed was that he was far more specific and astute and unforgiving in his criticism of his own work than I was.

I have not met a writer of any age who takes the gesture of writing for theatre more seriously than did Alistair McDowall in his early twenties and continues to do now.

It was, I think, shortly after I read *Jennifer Jane* that he gave me his new play *Brilliant Adventures* to read. I looked forward to reading it because I liked his first few plays.

I had no idea how extraordinary it was going to be.

It's a play that appears to start as an exquisite example of a familiar form. Two brothers fend off life in their Middlesbrough housing estate with compassion and wit and palpable love for one another. Their world is dislocated and violent. It is beautifully wrought and evokes the forty years of familiar social naturalistic playwriting that Edward Bond's *Saved* most famously articulated in the UK. And then something genuinely remarkable happens.

Alistair McDowall graced two genres together in a way I had never imagined: economic socio-naturalism and science fiction. He did it with astonishing understatement and skill.

I gave Chris Campbell, the literary manager of the Royal Court Theatre, a copy of the play. It felt like it must have felt in the early days of rock and roll as young Teds passed seven-inch singles to one another. It felt like an exchange of something culturally remarkable. Chris's enthusiasm for Ali's work has charged the last four years of his playwriting career.

My enthusiasm was as striking when I saw the Royal Court production of *Talk Show* in the Open Court repertory as part of Vicky Featherstone's first season as Artistic Director at the theatre. Or when I went with my son to see *Captain Amazing* at the Soho Theatre, both of us leaving the theatre with tears pouring down our face. Returning to read the play this evening left me in the same state.

In a sense, three of these plays, while beautifully directed and acted, deserved larger lives. They are significant plays and, if I know anything about playwriting, they will survive. But they were produced in small spaces or on short runs. It took the masterful *Pomona* for Ali to reach the attention he deserved. I saw it during its run at the Orange Tree in 2014. It was speedily and rightly acknowledged as one of the year's best plays and revived by the National Theatre the next year.

I had been saying for four years that Alistair McDowall had the potential to become the most significant voice of his generation. At last, other people were starting to say it, too.

The plays gathered in this collection share concerns or interests. The playwrights I love most tend to return to the obsessions in this way.

Each of Ali's plays reaches for a form that best articulates its content. This can result in the linguistic collapse of *Captain Amazing* or the chronological disruptions of *Brilliant Adventures* because such collapse and disruption best articulate his ideas.

He is the writer I know – indeed perhaps the person I know – with the most encyclopaedic knowledge of film history. What is striking for such a lover of film is that each of these plays is so theatrical. He writes for and with a love of the theatre. This manifests itself in a confidence of stagecraft and a brilliant eye for stage image. In these plays, Ali is writing fearlessly in three dimensions.

Something that surprises me about him in these plays and those others I have read, including those early plays and others as yet unproduced (Alistair is an excitingly prolific writer), is how each counterpoints originality of form and a fascination with genre. The science fiction of *Brilliant Adventures* is matched by the horror of the H.P. Lovecraft-inspired *Pomona* or the Marvel comic energy of *Captain Amazing*. Originality, Ali understands, doesn't exist solely in inventiveness, but in the tension between inventiveness and a command of form.

His concerns are thematic as much as they are formal.

Each of his plays counterpoints a startling flint and lack of sentimentality with a deep and felt compassion for his characters.

He writes men with particular incision and examines the heartbreak of watching fathers in despair with more clarity than many playwrights of his generation.

His rigorous examination of the dehumanising savagery of poverty is compelling.

His faith in, and frustration with, the English is as marked as his anger at economic inequality. It is an anger that never becomes didactic or even prescriptive. Rather, he continues to look with ferocity into the heart of economic darkness and write with urgency about what he finds there.

I think this political commitment and unsentimental humanity is why Ali's use of genre works so beautifully. He seems to understand that humans are defined by the stories that we tell one another about who we are. We exist in the spaces between the conventions of those stories and the peculiarities of our lives. In his plays, defined both by their compassion and their absurdity (a father chained up and trained as a dog on a leash, a driver circling the heart of hell on a Manchester ring road, a young man hosting a chat show from his own skint base-ment, a divorced father in a super-hero cape), he dramatises that space. He articulates that tension between the convention and the individual, the genre and the story, with more honesty and commitment to the form than any other playwright this millennium.

SIMON STEPHENS
2016

Introduction

Hi!

Thanks for buying this book, or borrowing it from someone, or just standing around in a shop reading it for a bit. I'm going to do my best to introduce the four plays in here as best I can. I am now on attempt four of writing this introduction, after several ill-advised versions that were endless, tedious exercises in autobiography that no one asked for, so instead I'll try and get to the point . . .

The four plays in this collection bridge the point at which I became a full-time writer. *Brilliant Adventures* and *Captain Amazing* were written when I was still working as a gallery attendant in a Manchester art gallery, *Talk Show* was the first play I wrote after becoming a writer full-time, and *Pomona* was written the same year the other three plays were first staged. It's a bit of an odd mix as the first three seem closely linked in theme and content, and the fourth is quite different. I tend to write quite quickly, so there are plays in between these that would make the transition seem less jarring than it might reading these four in a row, but those ones haven't made it onto the stage as of the time of writing.

*

Spoilers Ho!
If you haven't read the plays yet,
avoid this part of the introduction until you have.

*

Brilliant Adventures was written in 2010, when I was still working at the gallery, occasionally doing tours but mostly just standing around telling people not to touch things. A lot of my days were spent not doing much, so I kept a notebook in my pocket and planned my play, then did the bulk of the writing on days off, evenings and weekends.

It was the play that became my kind of calling card, and I think just about every theatre in the UK read it at some point.

It was the play that first introduced me to the Royal Court, National Theatre, and many others I'm lucky enough to still be working with. Then in 2011 it won one of the Bruntwood awards. On the day, Maxine Peake handed me a cheque for £8,000 and I could leave my day job. Which was exceptional timing as I'd just lost my day job the night before.

(To this day I feel a bit odd on the rare occasions I bump into Maxine – I realise it wasn't her money, but since she was the one who gave me the cheque I'll always feel kind of in debt to her, and also worried she might ask for it back at some point.)

When you write a play about a flat on an abandoned housing estate with a time machine in it, you get asked quite a lot where the idea came from. I honestly have no idea. It never seemed unusual to me, it was just part of the fabric of the story. The closest I've ever come to explaining the sensation of an idea cropping up is by using a clumsy analogy about finding your keys: when you find your keys, they're always somewhere you put them, and so the feeling when you eventually find them isn't one of discovery but one of 'Oh, of course they're there.' If I'm writing and a moment arrives that feels right for the play, I'll kind of have the same sensation. So with *Adventures*, I had this idea about two brothers and this abandoned estate, and then – oh, of course, one of them's built a time machine. Things feel right or they don't. Eventually I'll work out they feel right because they're speaking from somewhere deeper in the play than the surface of the plot or the characters, and are a way into writing what sits underneath everything else.

I grew up in a small village in North Yorkshire about a twenty-minute drive from Middlesbrough. A lot of my mates lived in Marton, which is a suburb of Boro, and so I spent a lot of my weekends kicking around Middlesbrough's town centre growing up. Despite not living actually within it, Boro's always seemed like my home town as it's the only place near where I grew up that anyone's actually ever heard of; although usually for bad reasons. Middlesbrough has often appeared in the news to document drug problems, the closing down of industry, or decaying estates that have been left to crumble to dust.

When I decided to write a play set on an abandoned estate in Middlesbrough, I wanted to be extremely careful about how I was handling it – I didn't want it to be yet another play dramatising a version of things being 'grim up north'. *Adventures* looks like one of those plays at first – when the lights come up we recognise the scruffy-looking flat set – but then spends the rest of its running time pulling that all to pieces. The plot is concerned with some of the things about the town that make it into the news, but it has a story set apart from that too. I've always been aware of the unspoken rule that certain areas are only allowed certain stories, and I hoped *Adventures* could push against that a tiny bit. Middlesbrough has its problems – but it also has an amazing warmth and brilliantly caustic sense of humour. It's a place with a very defined personality. I hope the play reflects that to some extent.

*

Captain Amazing was written after *Adventures* but opened just before it, at Live Theatre in Newcastle, where it was developed. I wrote an introduction to the playtext when it was first published, so I won't repeat myself with how it was developed – instead we've put that introduction after the play in this book.

*

Talk Show was written in 2012, and opened at the Royal Court in the summer of 2013, as part of Vicky Featherstone's first big gesture as artistic director – Open Court. The play was staged as part of a six-play cycle, all performed by the same rep company of actors. I can't begin to write about the play without first talking about the tragedy that surrounded the first production of it. Paul Bhattacharjee, one of the actors in the rep company, died during the rehearsals for *Talk Show*.

After Paul didn't arrive for rehearsals his part was recast, and we ultimately heard the news after the second performance of the show.

I had only had chance to say 'Hello' to him during the meet and greet on the first day, but I found myself in the middle of a huge amount of grief and sadness and confusion, with nothing of use to say to anyone about any of it. It was a horrible and bizarre time.

I didn't know Paul at all, but through talking to anyone who ever knew him it's obvious how loved he was – everyone had a story about how kind he was, how brilliant an actor he was, the various amazing things he'd been involved in throughout his life.

All I could do then, and all I can do now, is apologise for having so little to say about such a terrible loss.

*

Talk Show feels, whenever I return to it, like my most personal play. Which I immediately want to cross out as a statement, as they're *all* very personal. So what I think I mean is that the lead character is the most like me of any of my characters.

I didn't intend that to happen – I'm usually desperately trying to avoid it – but I remember watching the show one night, and listening to Sam's long meltdown at the end and realising it was just me on stage, venting my various insecurities and anxieties to a paying audience. It still feels almost comically raw to me.

It's also probably the most straightforward play in the collection – it's pretty much naturalism, it's a family play, it's a version of a particular kind of American family play – but it still plays with form in a way that links it to the other plays. The use of the canned laughter and applause, when employed well, does a strange thing to the feeling of the room – after Sam tells one of his terrible jokes and there's audible laughter, there's usually a beat before the audience laugh themselves, at the laughter. As the play goes on, the real and fake laughter will sometimes kick in at the same time, and sometimes there'll be a delay. The audience might join in with the applause at certain points too, which starts to do a weird thing with the fourth wall. Sam is talking to the audience, but an audience that isn't there – but they are there, as this is a play. The effect makes the audience feel both involved and implicated, and voyeuristic at the same time (I hope . . .). The play is then traditional in form overall, but with a disruptive spirit that matches the characters, and with a fourth wall that's not made of bricks.

*

The first three plays in this collection feel like they share the most in common with one another. They're all filled with characters who struggle to articulate themselves, either through anxiety or other problems. They all play some kind of game with the audience – the talk show in *Talk Show*, the character switching in *Captain Amazing*, and the biggest one: the cardboard box in *Brilliant Adventures* that the audience collectively agrees to believe is a time machine.

The biggest similarity I think, though, is that they're all preoccupied with what happens when women leave the picture. The boys in *Brilliant Adventures* are a pack of lost boys, seeming much younger than they are. The central character in *Captain Amazing* briefly flourishes out of his passivity when women enter his life. And the men in *Talk Show* all seem completely unable to make ends meet or even express basic emotions once the women in their lives leave.

They also share a shifting relationship between fantasy and reality. The fantasy in each play either exists in fantastic onstage elements (time machines) or as escape for characters from their own heads, which then bleeds out into the real world (superheroes and talk shows). The next play also toys with fantasy, but in darker realms than the previous three.

*

Pomona is a real place. A lot of people who saw the play thought I'd made it up, but it's in Manchester, it's on the tram line, it's slap bang in the middle of the city.

I'd been haunted by it for a long time, this funny little overgrown island surrounded by roads and canals and rails – not unlike the setting for J.G. Ballard's *Concrete Island*. The street lights have never worked there in my experience – so at night it's an inky blackness that appears as though someone forgot to fill the rest of the city in.

As I write this, it's in the process of changing into somewhere less mysterious. Despite a local campaign to turn it into a park, it's to be the site for new expensive flats.

Though it's sad to lose the place itself, it doesn't matter so much to me that the play will be geographically out of date – and as I said, people just thought I'd made the place up anyway.

Pomona is a play that could take place in any major city in the UK. It's not about Pomona, that's just a place for the play to circle and prowl. It's a play about my own fears and anxieties made incarnate. It's a play about cities written by someone who spends vast amounts of time travelling between two major ones. It's a play about the first decade-and-a-bit of the twenty-first century. Too much internet and coffee. Too much information. All of it crippling. The characters consume frantically and are ultimately consumed themselves.

It was a surprise to me that the play connected with as many people as it seemed to – I thought it was so insular and bleak it would mostly alienate people. I wrote it during a bad patch and, reading it again, I think it wears its mood on its sleeve.

Despite seeming quite different on the surface to the other three, *Pomona* is, like the others, a play about lost people. The difference being the characters in the previous plays have some awareness of how they came to be lost – in *Pomona* it's just a by-product of contemporary life.

Searching for other connections between this play and the others, I think they all sit quite neatly within genres – if not the ones I think they first appear to be. Despite featuring sci-fi elements, *Brilliant Adventures* is more of a western – an abandoned and lawless estate is thrown into further danger with the arrival of an outsider. *Captain Amazing* has obvious superhero connotations but it's written more like a children's play, with one character performing a cast of thousands in short snatches. *Talk Show* is absolutely in the tradition of the American family play, which is a genre in itself, and *Pomona*, despite all the horror elements, is a detective story without the detective – the audience fills that role themselves.

As a side note, I'd add that Ned, the original director, swapped out the Rubik's Cubes in the text for dice, which I think was a really smart way of tying the events of the game and the rest of the play together very cleanly, if you prefer to read it that way.

*

Thanks again for buying/borrowing/reading; I truly appreciate every bit of support I've had for my writing from childhood to now. So here's a short list of people I have to thank, as this book wouldn't exist without them:

The casts and creative teams of all these plays were all an absolute joy and inspiration to work with, without exception.

In alphabetical order, Ned Bennett, Clive Judd and Caroline Steinbeis directed these plays and gave me notes on each that improved them immeasurably, and continue to have impact on every play I write.

Other people who helped me hugely with redrafting each of these, again in alphabetical order: Suzanne Bell, Leo Butler, Gez Casey, Chris Campbell, Vicky Featherstone, Sarah Frankcom, Carissa Hope Lynch, Simon Stephens, Nils Tabert.

The theatres that produced each of these plays throughout their runs: Live Theatre, National Theatre, Orange Tree, Royal Court, Royal Exchange, Royal Welsh College of Music and Drama.

Thanks to Peter Moore, Stu Kiesow and Steep Theatre Chicago for letting me use their beautiful image from their production of *Brilliant Adventures* for the cover.

Thanks to Anna Brewer and Bloomsbury Methuen Drama for continuing to publish my work.

A special thanks to my agent Howard Gooding for years of support, guidance, and friendship.

To Simon Stephens for being my mate and theatre big brother for years, always being available when I've gotten stuck with anything. And more than likely helping shift a few tickets with his very vocal support of these plays.

To Jan Hunter and the sadly missed Davod Hunter, two teachers I'd never be able to repay for the encouragement and tools they gave me at key points during my childhood and adolescence.

To my family for always supporting my terrible financial decision to pursue a career as a writer, and for sitting through these plays which I know aren't really your thing.

And I dedicate this collection as a whole to my wife Amy, for being everything I could never hope to put into words.

ALISTAIR MCDOWALL

2016

Brilliant Adventures

for sean, lizzie, and callum
and
for the north-east, and the people there
THE N.W.R.A.

Brilliant Adventures was first performed at the Royal Exchange, Manchester, on 8 May 2013 in a co-production between the Royal Exchange and Live Theatre, Newcastle, with the following cast and creatives:

Luke   Robert Lonsdale/Lee Armstrong
Rob   Joseph Arkley
Greg   Ian Bonar
Ben   Laurence Mitchell
The Man   Michael Hodgson

Director   Caroline Steinbeis
Designer   Max Jones
Lighting Designer   Kay Haynes
Sound and Music   Richard Hammarton

Characters

Luke, *nineteen, anxious, irritable*
Rob, *twenty-six, energetic, quick-tempered, never seen without his baseball cap on*
Greg, *eighteen, glasses, talkative*
Ben, *thirty-two, well-dressed, calm, confident*
The Man, *forties*

Setting

A council flat in Middlesbrough.

Time

2010.

Notes

A question without a question mark denotes a flatness of tone.

A dash (–) indicates an interruption of speech or train of thought.

An ellipsis (. . .) indicates either a trailing off, a breather, a shift, or a transition.

An oblique (/) indicates where the next line of dialogue interrupts or overlaps, thus:

Here, **A** and **B** speak simultaneously:

A   / Nice to meet you.
B   Nice to meet you.

Here, **B** interrupts **A**:

A   Nice to / meet you.
B   Nice to meet you.

Act One

One

A small council flat. The ground floor of a converted house.

Across the back wall is the front door with several locks and an intercom, a serving hatch and doorway to a small kitchen, a small table and two chairs. On the table is a large goldfish bowl with a fish in it. There are also hundreds and hundreds of books and a tower of DVDs stacked from the floor up.

Stage left is a doorway to the bedroom and bathroom; stage right is the window, which has curtains tightly drawn. Leaning against the wall next to the window is a single mattress and a rolled-up duvet. Downstage centre is a tired-looking sofa and a television with DVD player balanced precariously on top.

Downstage left is a tall cardboard box, perhaps from a fridge-freezer, standing on end. There is a door flap cut into one side, and on the other are several cardboard dials and switches.

Luke *is lying on the sofa, playing a Gameboy.*

The intercom buzzes.

Beat.

He gets up and goes over to it; it buzzes again before he can get there.

Hang on.

He presses the button.

H-hello?

Intercom   Lerrus in!

He presses a button, then opens the door and sticks his head out.

(*Off.*) What are you doin?

Greg (*off*)   Is that your horse out there?

Luke comes back in and goes back to the sofa. **Greg** *follows, holding a pizza box. He shuts the door behind him. During the following he goes to the kitchen, gets a knife and fork, then sits down on the floor near* **Luke** *and eats the chicken parmesan out of the pizza box.*

Luke   What?

Greg   Is that your horse out the front?

Luke   Why would I have a . . . horse?

Greg   There's a horse knocking about outside your door.

Luke   There's loads of em round here.

Greg   Thought it was gonna charge me.

Luke   Ch-charge you?

Greg   Head-butt me or sommit. People get killed by horses all the time, they stomp on you and that.

He stuffs a huge forkful of parmo in his mouth.

Greg *(with mouth full)*   Vywaa aah, ohrss. *('Violent as, horses.')*

Luke   Can I have . . . a bit?

Greg   No you can't, man, I'm starving. And I had to bloody nick a fiver off me dad to get this.

Luke   Just a bit.

Greg   You can have one chip.

Luke *(taking a chip)*   Tight . . . bastard.

He grabs a handful of chips before **Greg** *can stop him and dashes back to his seat, triumphant.*

Greg   Bastard! Cost us four pound, this. And I nearly got killed on me way to get it.

Luke   B . . . bollocks.

Greg   I did an all! Scallies hoying bricks at us all the way there. They're all stood up in them crumbly houses opposite Pizza

Zeus chucking bits of the buildings about. Fucking outrageous, man. Using the buildings as weapons now.

Luke   Just . . . cross the road.

He goes back to his Gameboy.

Beat.

Greg   Is your brother comin round today?

Luke   Dunno.

Greg   I've got to ask him sommit.

Luke   He's not . . . interested.

Greg   How'd you know he's not interested? He might – How do you know?

Luke   I just know he's not.

Greg   How though?

Luke   Cos he calls you a specky fucking . . . cunt all day.

Greg   That doesn't mean he's not interested. Don't have to be friends to be business partners.

Luke   He doesn't want you as his business partner.

Greg   I can be valuable, me.

Luke   You'd be . . . shit.

Greg   No, I wouldn't.

Luke   You would.

Greg   No, I wouldn't, I'd be alright.

Luke   You can't even hack little d-dickheads . . . chucking stuff at you.

Greg   That's different – And they weren't little either, they were like our size.

Maybe even bigger.

Luke   You'd get knifed in five . . . minutes.

Greg   Well, I wouldn't be on my own first, would I? I'd be like an apprentice first.

Luke   Apprentice . . .

Greg   Like Rob's helper or sommit.

Luke   What've you got to offer? You can't f-fight, you can't do maths –

Greg   I've got GCSEs.

Luke   Shit GCSEs.

Greg   More than your Rob's got.

Luke   He's got other – talents.

Greg   I can contribute.

Luke   What with?

Pause.

Greg   Enthusiasm. Motivation. I want to climb the ladder. The ladder of *business*.

Luke   There's no . . . ladder. There's just rungs. And no . . . outer bit. The outer bit of the ladder. So the rungs aren't . . . attached to owt.

Greg   What?

Luke   It's a metaphor. For something. I guess.

Greg   Shit metaphor.

Luke *goes back to his Gameboy.*

Beat.

Greg   What you playing?

Luke   T-Tetris.

Greg   Bit old-school that, like.

Luke   It's a classic.

Pause.

Greg *has finished with his parmo.*

Greg   Can I have a go?

Luke   I'm playing.

Greg   Well, it's a bit rude.

Luke   Why?

Greg   Cos. You've got a guest round. It's rude to your guest. Just sat playing Tetris and not talking to us.

Luke   You're here all the time.

Greg   I'm still your guest. (*Beat.*) It's very rude.

Pause.

He gets up and walks around the room. He looks at the fish bowl.

Have you fed Proust?

Luke   Yes.

Greg (*scrutinising the fish*)   He looks thin.

Luke   Fish can't look thin.

Greg   He does though.

Luke   D-don't feed him.

Greg   I'm not.

Luke   If you overfeed him, he'll . . . die.

Greg   I know.

Beat.

Did you think about what I was saying yesterday?

Luke   N-no.

Greg   You didn't think?

Luke   You're . . . not moving in here.

Greg   Aw come on, man.

Luke   It's a one-bedroom . . . flat.

Greg   I can just kip on the sofa, here.

Luke   *I* sleep in here.

Greg   You sleep on the mattress, I can sleep on the sofa.

Luke   No.

Greg   Why not?

Luke   I like . . . living on my own.

Greg   Please, man . . .

Luke   What do you wanna live here for, anyway? You sh-shit yourself every time you have to w-walk here.

Greg   I'll get used to it. And I won't even go out. You never go out.

Luke   You're not moving . . . in.

Beat.

You can k-kip over when you want, but you're not living here.

Greg   Can I tonight?

Luke   No.

Greg   You just said when I want!

Luke   You're not – You'll never leave. You'll just k-keep saying that every night.

Greg   I won't!

Luke   You will. Just pack it in. Stop . . . talking about it. I only just moved out on my . . . own. Need my space.

Beat.

Greg *stands up and heads to the bathroom.*

Greg   I'm trying to make a better life, man. I'm trying to do sommit right and, and, and, *develop* myself. And you won't even let us kip on your sofa. *And* you won't even put in a good word for me with your brother –

Luke   How can I p-put in a good word for you? He *knows* you.

Greg   No friend at all, you.

He exits.

(*Off.*)   No friend at all!

The buzzer goes.

Luke *gets up to answer it, muttering.*

Luke   H-h –

Intercom   Let us in you stuttering dickhead.

Luke   Y-you didn't say you were coming r-r –

Intercom Stop / gibbering and press the fucking button.

Luke   You, you, no, you – Fine.

He presses the button, then opens the door and goes back to the sofa.

Enter **Rob***. On a dog lead he has* **The Man***, a wild-looking middle-aged man.*

The Man *walks on all fours and is naked except for a filthy pair of shorts, a bumbag, some filthy socks, gloves, and a red scarf around his neck. During the following,* **Rob** *ties* **The Man***'s lead to the door knob and he scutters around for a bit before settling on the floor.*

Rob   I need to make an appointment now?

Luke   N –

Rob   You don't want to see us now you've moved into your fancy flat in Cracktown?

Luke   I need to – I have to do work.

Rob   Oh yeah, you look busy, like.

Luke   I'm having a . . . break.

Rob   I'm only dropping in.

Luke   Need my . . . p-privacy.

The toilet flushes.

Rob   Oh, aye. Privacy.

Enter **Greg**, *doing his fly.*

Rob   This cock's welcome and I'm not?

Greg   Alright, Rob?

Rob (*eating* **Greg***'s parmo*)   I'm having the rest of your parmo.

Greg   Aw, come on, man. I had to rob me own dad for that.

Rob   That's why you don't deserve it.

Greg   I was gonna eat that an all.

Rob   Has he told you why he doesn't want me round any more?

Luke   I didn't –

Greg   He doesn't want me here either, Rob.

Rob   Well, I can understand why he wouldn't want a stack of sausage-dog shite like you here, but why wouldn't he want this handsome cunt round?

Rob *grabs* **Luke***'s head roughly and kisses his cheek.*

During the following, **Greg** *goes and pats* **The Man** *on the head.*

Luke   Gerroff –

Rob   I like to check up on you, living in this fucking wasteland.

Luke   I'm fine.

Rob   Surprised you've even got electricity –

Luke   It's n-not –

Rob   – Fucking knobheads keep nicking the wire from the power stations.

You don't even have the curtains open. Smackheads making faces at you?

Luke   Will you . . . calm down. You're exhausting.

Rob   Alright, alright, alright. Alright.

He sits down on the sofa next to **Luke**.

He starts rolling a cigarette.

Rob   Fuck knows why you want to live round here though, being like you are. Living where I do all my business.

Greg   / Rob, about –

Rob   Can I smoke in here, or is that not allowed either?

Luke   You know you . . . can.

Rob *lights his fag. He goes over to the serving hatch, where there's a little ashtray.*

Greg   / Rob –

Rob   It's not the sort of place someone like you should be living.

Luke   S-s-someone –

Rob   Someone like you. Someone who jumps at his own shadow. You'll have a fucking seizure if they knock on your window.

Luke   I'm n-not that . . . bad.

Rob   This is a dealer's flat, man. You're living in a dealer's flat.

Luke   It's . . . not.

Rob   Course it is. It's fucking custom-built.

Window in the bog goes right out in the alley –

Greg (*nodding sagely*)   Right out in the back, yeah.

Rob   Grilles on the front door, main window here overlooking the – well, not the green. The brown.

Luke   Stop – coveting my flat.

He gets up and tidies away **Greg**'s *pizza box.*

Rob   I'm just saying, that's what it's made for. Not for living in.

There's not anyone lives on this estate that isn't hooked on sommit.

Greg   Ha, yeah.

Rob   Even the cameras can't get you, cos of the angle. / It's perfect.

Greg   Yeah, I noticed that, Rob. / Noticed the CCTV.

Luke (*returning*)   It's my flat. You're not using it.

Rob   I know. (*Beat.*) Just saying.

Luke   Well, don't. Don't be just saying.

Rob   Alright.

Beat.

Greg   Rob –

Rob   How about if I moved in?

Greg   He doesn't want people moving in, Rob –

Rob   I can pay rent, dickhead. Unlike you.

Luke   No one's . . . moving in. Moved to get away f-from all your . . . shite –

Rob   Oh, so you moved *here*?

Luke   I just moved where the council p-put us. Disability doesn't pay that m-much.

Rob   Disability – What disability have you got, anyway?

Luke   F-f-fucking obvious . . . isn't it?

Rob   Having a mong voice doesn't make you a mong.

Luke   Ch-ch . . .

Rob   You talk the talk but you don't walk the walk.

Luke   – Charming.

Luke *glances out of the curtains, keeping them tightly shut.*

Greg   Rob –

Rob   Look at the state of you though.

Luke   What?

Rob   Terrified.

Luke   I'm . . . fine.

Rob   You're shit scared of your own estate.

Luke   I'm f-f-f –

Rob   If I lived here you wouldn't be scared.

Luke   If you were . . . here you'd be dealing out my l-living room.

Rob   I'd be discreet.

Luke   Discreet? Dragging . . . him around?

Rob   You know, you're pretty fucking ungrateful considering I paid for everything in here.

Greg   Aw, let's not / start –

Rob   I bought this. And this. And those. And that. And the fucking keks you're wearing too.

Luke   I'm not . . . talking about –

Rob   Place would be bare if it weren't for my money –

Greg   / Come on –

Luke   I-I –

Rob   You don't like where it comes from, but you'll take whatever you can get.

Luke   L-let me *speak*.

Beat.

Rob   Sorry. Sorry.

Beat.

Luke   I'm . . . grateful. For your help. But I want to live on my own n-now, and I want to live without . . . your s-stuff going on all the t-time so I can . . . focus on my work.

Makes me n-nervous.

Beat.

Rob   Alright, sorry. Just fucking around.

Luke *nods.*

Rob   Sorry.

Pause.

Rob *stubs out his cigarette and takes a huff from his asthma inhaler.*

He kicks **The Man** *gently.*

The Man *groans.*

Rob   Don't be falling asleep. We're leaving in a bit.

Lazy fucker.

He coughs.

Greg   Rob . . .

Rob   What?

Greg   Have you had a think about what I was asking?

Rob   No I haven't, Greg.

Greg   You haven't?

Rob   I don't need to think about whether I should give you any work, that's a fucking obvious no.

Luke   T-t- / told you.

Greg   Did you not have a look at my CV?

Rob   Why would I want to read your fucking CV?

Greg   For my references.

Rob   Oh aye, your references. Your schoolteachers. I can tell what they'll say: 'Gregory is a useless dickend who can't tell shite from sherbet.'

Greg   They wouldn't say that, man.

Rob   They'd say worse probably, looking at your string of fucking 'F's and 'U's.

Stop putting CVs through my door.

Greg   Least I've *got* GCSEs.

Rob   Yeah, well. Glad you've got that for comfort. What with being a specky . . . shrimpy . . . smelly little wank-addict, you need something to keep your self-esteem up.

Greg   I'm not a wank-addict!

Luke   / L . . . leave him –

Rob   I'm giving you an excuse calling you an addict. If you're not then why the fuck were you wanking on my sofa?

Greg   You said you weren't gonna talk about that again!

Luke   / Come on . . .

Rob   How can I not talk about it? No one can sit on that sofa any more.

Greg   I didn't . . . It was the middle . . . I was just . . . Aw, fuck the pair of yous.

He springs up and goes for the door.

Luke   I d-didn't / . . .

Greg   You're not standing up for us. Yous can both fuck off.

He leaves, slamming the door behind him.

Beat.

Rob   He's a laugh, him, isn't he?

Luke   You shouldn't –

Rob   He's alright, he knows I'm taking the piss.

Luke   He's got a weak . . . c-constitution.

The buzzer goes.

See, he's back . . . already.

Rob *goes to the intercom before* **Luke** *can get up.*

Rob *(into intercom)*   Yeah?

Intercom *(muffled speech).*

Rob *(into intercom)*   In a sec, yeah.

He opens the front door.

Luke   Who's that?

Rob   A mate.

Rob *leaves.*

Luke   A m-m –

Before **Luke** *can go and look,* **Rob** *comes back in with a plastic bag and shuts the door.*

Rob *(kicking* **The Man***)*   Come on, daft arse, we're off.

Luke   What are you . . . d-doing?

Rob   Nowt –

Luke   Y-y-y-y –

Rob   He's just giving us my CDs back –

Luke *goes to grab the bag*

Rob   It's just my CDs, mate –

Luke   You don't h-have a-any . . . / CDs –

Rob   Just leave it –

Luke   You . . . said you were gonna . . . not do –

Rob   It's just this one time, man. Had to be quick.

Luke   Now some fucking . . .s-s-*psycho* knows where I . . . live –

Rob   He's not a psycho, he's a mate.

Beat.

Luke   You fucking bastard man.

Rob   Luke –

Luke   You said. You *said*.

Rob   Calm down.

Luke   You –

Rob   I won't do it again.

Luke   It's . . . not the point, you –

Rob   Listen. *Listen*.

A bloke I know has bought the flat upstairs, so it won't affect you.

We'll be using up there now.

Beat.

Luke   Upstairs?

Rob   I've met this bloke from London. Fucking wadded.

We're going to work together –

Luke   W-why's he –

Rob   He needs someone with connections round here, so
he's investing in me.

Help us expand and everything.

Luke   And he's living up . . . stairs?

Rob   He's not *living* up there, he's using it to work out of.

Luke   And you –

Rob   I didn't – It's coincidence. *Coincidence.*

This is good news for us man – The amount of money he's got –

We can have a fresh start.

Luke   It's n-not a f-f-fresh start if y-you're still doing the . . .
same sh-*shite* –

Luke *is wandering around his flat.*

Rob   We won't be interrupting your precious experiments,
alright?

Luke   No, but you'll be . . . f-filling the building with
f-f-fucking . . . smackheads.

Rob   We have to have a base here, it's the main marketplace
for fuck's sake –

Luke   This is where I live!

Blackout.

Two

The same. A few days later. **Greg** *lies on the sofa, playing the Gameboy.*
Pause.

Greg (*muttering*)   Fucking bent block bastard . . .

Pause.

There's a knock at the door.

Greg *looks up. He stands up. He looks down the hall.*

Greg   Luke, man.

Beat.

Luke man, door.

Beat.

Greg *goes and opens the door.* **Ben** *is standing in the hall.*

Greg   Ello?

Ben   Hi. I'm supposed to meet Rob here.

Greg   Oh right, yeah. (*Beat.*) Do you wanna come in like?

Ben   Thank you.

He walks into the flat. **Greg** *shuts the door.*

Ben   Ben, good to meet you.

Ben *shakes* **Greg***'s hand.*

Greg   I'm Greg, me.

Ben   Oh – I thought – Luke? Luke lives here?

Greg   Yeah, he does. I think he's just having a shit at the
minute.

Have a sit down and that.

Ben *sits on the sofa.* **Greg** *sits on the opposite arm.*

Pause.

Greg I'd make you a brew, but Luke doesn't drink tea or owt, so he's not got none of the equipment.

Beat.

Ben Do you live here too?

Greg Naw . . . Well. Mebbes soon, but not just yet.

I'm just trying to sort out my business situation at the moment, like.

Ben What do you do?

Greg Well, nowt at the moment. That's why I need to sort it out.

Ben Ah.

Greg I'm most likely going into business with Rob.

Ben Oh?

Greg Aye, we're just working out some things at the moment. He's going over my CV, checking my background, you know.

Ben He asked for your CV?

Greg Well, naw. But I give him it anyway. Showing initiative and that.

Ben Right.

Pause.

Greg Are you in business with him, then?

Ben I'm putting some money forward.

Greg You're . . . *investing* in him?

Ben I suppose.

Greg Well, mebbes we'll be working together then.

Ben Maybe.

Greg *nods.*

Pause.

Greg Are you from London?

Ben *nods.*

Greg What's it like down there? Dead posh?

Ben Some of it. Some of it not.

Greg Bet it's posher than up here.

Ben Some of it. Some of it not.

Greg You've got quite a posh voice.

Ben I think most accents sound posh here.

Beat.

Greg What are you doing up here, like?

Ben Lots of reasons. Money reasons.

Greg Oh right, yeah. Shrink your overheads and that.

Ben Something like that.

Greg They're always saying that Boro's got, like, the cheapest houses and that. And drugs. And prozzies. People say that.

Ben Seems so.

Greg Not like that's a good thing though. Houses round here are all manky.

Ben Do you live round here?

Greg I live close like, but not right here. I live somewheres a bit nicer. Not that much nicer, but not as dodge as round here.

Ben Right, yes.

Pause.

Greg   Have you got loads of money, like?

Ben   I –

Greg   I'm not being rude or owt, just asking. I'm not like, asking you for any.

Ben   No.

Greg   I'm just asking.

Ben   Right.

Greg   As a businessman.

Ben   Yes.

Greg   A businessman asking a businessman.

Ben   Okay.

Beat.

Greg   So do yous then?

Ben   I . . . I've got enough.

Greg   Enough?

Ben   Yes.

Greg   Enough for what?

Ben   Enough . . . to buy most of round here.

Greg   Most of what?

Ben   Just most of it.

Beat.

Greg *grins.*

Greg   Waww! You're fucking well loaded then!

Ben   I do alright.

Greg   Have you got mansions and that?

Ben   What?

Greg   Have you got a mint car or something? A Ferrari?

Ben   I'm not really . . . into things like that.

Greg   You're like, pretty young though, aren't you?

Ben   I suppose.

Greg   How old are you?

Ben   I'm thirty-two.

Greg   Aw, that's not that young then. (*Beat.*) What's your secret?

Ben   My *secret*?

Greg   Yeah, what's your secret?

How can I, as a businessman just starting out, get proper rich like you?

Ben   I . . . I don't – There's not so much a –

Greg   Howay mate, do us a favour. I wanna be like you.

Pause.

Ben   You just have to . . .

Beat.

You have to stop . . . *romanticising* people.

Greg   Right.

Ben   People aren't so important.

Greg   No, no. Yeah. Yes. Very interesting.

Beat.

Makes sense. People. Hm.

The buzzer goes.

Greg *gets up to answer it.*

Greg   I'll remember that. This'll probably be Rob now. (*Into intercom.*) Alright, Rob?

Intercom   Open the door you fucking dickhead.

Greg (*pressing button and opening door*)   Haha, sounds like him.

Enter **Rob***, with* **The Man***.*

Greg   Alright R –

Rob *pushes* **Greg** *out the door so hard he flies into the wall outside –*

Greg   Aw come –

– and then slams the door. There is immediately knocking and whining from outside.

Ben *stands up.*

Rob   He bothering you?

Ben   No, no. Just talking.

Rob   Yeah, that's all he fucking ever does is talk.

Ben   He said he'll be working for you.

Rob   Well, I think that'd be pretty obvious bollocks. Do you want a brew?

Ben   He said there's no –

Rob (*fishing in pockets*)   Aye, it's alright. I bring me own tea bags.

You'd think he'd have some in for visitors, like.

The Man *is whining at the noise outside.*

Rob *clips him round the ear.*

Rob   Shut it. You want to be out with him?

He goes to the kitchen to make the tea.

Ben *watches* **The Man***.*

Rob   What was he talking to you about?

Ben   Money, mostly.

Rob   He didn't beg any off you, did he?

Ben   No.

Rob   Well. Tell me if he does. You'll be seeing a lot of him if you're here.

He hasn't got anyone else so hangs round day and night.

Ben   Right.

Enter **Luke***, who's clearly just had a shower.*

Rob   Here's the man of the house.

Luke   W . . .

Ben (*stretching a hand out*)   Ben. Good to meet you.

Luke   . . .

Rob   He's not very good talking to people he doesn't know, like.

Luke *hears the noise at the door and goes to open it.*

Rob   Aw don't, man.

Luke *opens the door and* **Greg** *stumbles in.*

Greg   That's not on, that.

Luke *shuts the door.*

Greg   You can't just be throwing people around like that, man. You knacked my back in, then.

Rob   Look, do you wanna brew or not?

Greg   Wh – Did I ask for a brew?

Rob   Do you want one?

Beat.

Greg   Yeah. If you're making one. That'd be class.

Rob   Right.

Luke   Y-y- / y –

Greg   Ben just told us his business secret –

Rob   Leave him alone.

Greg   / I'm not – I am –

Luke   Y . . .

Ben   It's alright.

Greg   See?

Luke   . . . You . . .

Rob   Spit it out.

Luke *frowns.*

Rob *hands* **Greg** *and* **Ben** *their tea.* **Greg***'s is in a bowl. This seems normal to him.*

They watch **Luke** *trying to speak.*

Luke   Y . . . ou're y-y-using my h . . . ouse as . . . a . . . m-meeting . . . r-room –

Rob   No we're not, man. I just wanted to introduce you, since you'll be neighbours.

Ben   Well. Not quite neighbours. Something like that.

He stretches his hand out.

Start again?

Beat.

Luke *shakes* **Ben***'s hand.*

Rob   He's alright, is Luke. He's just a bit protective about his new flat.

Ben   I would be too; living round here.

Rob   He was living in a decent area before.

Greg   He was living with you, Rob.

Rob   That's what I mean, gobshite. He was living with me and he chose to move out to fucking . . . round here.

Ben   Do you have a job, Luke?

Luke *shakes head.*

Greg   He's on benefits. Cos of his voice and his funny turns and that.

Rob   Let him speak for himself.

Luke   Y –

Greg   He's a proper genius, too.

Luke *looks furiously uncomfortable.*

Ben   A genius?

Rob   Aye, he's a fucking megabrain. Maths and science and everything.

Read all these.

Greg   And he didn't even get his GCSEs.

Luke   I . . . didn't –

Rob   He thinks exams are pointless, so he refused to even do em.

Ben   Right.

Greg   So he's a genius, but he does daft stuff like that, and he's also got his speaking thing and his funny turns. He's like that Good Will Hunting.

Luke   St-stop s-saying I'm like . . . Good Will Hunting. / All y-you ever s-say . . .

Greg   You are a bit like it though, man.

Ben   So what do you do with your time, Luke?

Luke *shrugs.*

Ben   You must have a lot of free time. What do you do?

Greg (*pointing at the cardboard box*)   He built that.

Beat.

Ben   The box?

Rob   It's not just a box.

Ben   It's not?

Luke *starts pleading with them not to say anything.*

Ben   What is it then?

Luke   It's n-n –

Rob   Don't be modest, man.

Greg   It's a time machine.

Luke *gives up in exasperation and sits down, defeated.*

Beat.

Ben   It's a time machine?

Rob *and* **Greg** *nod.*

Pause.

Ben *goes over to look at it.*

Ben   It's a box.

Greg   It's a time machine.

Ben   Is this a – a Middlesbrough joke I'm not supposed to get?

Rob   Stick your head in.

Ben   Are you having me on?

Greg   Have a look in it, man.

Luke   D-don-don't –

Ben *sticks his head in.*

Pause.

Ben   Jesus . . .

Greg   Told you.

Ben *comes back out.*

Pause.

Ben   This is . . .

Pause.

A *working* time machine?

Greg   Luke *made* it, man. He's a genius.

Luke   S-stop / *saying* . . . that –

Rob   He's like Rain Man or something. He just works this shit out.

Luke   Y-you c-can't . . . / tell anyo –

Ben   What have you done with it?

Beat.

Luke   N . . . nothing.

Beat.

Ben   Nothing?

Luke   It just . . . s-sits there.

Beat.

Ben   So you've built a working time machine, and you haven't used it?

Luke *shakes his head.*

Greg   Bit daft, isn't it?

Ben   How do you know it works?

Luke I just . . . kn-know.

Ben But how?

Luke I know.

Rob He's done the maths and that.

Greg He can't build one that gets you back, like. So if you go somewhere in it, you can't get back. Cos it just takes you, and not the machine.

Rob He's not *that* clever, eh?

Ben So you haven't – (*He laughs.*) You haven't done the lottery? Or, I don't – Bought stocks, or, or, *something*?

Greg You'd have to live everything again.

Ben But what's a week? You can live a week again. If it means millions.

Greg I thought you already had mill –

Rob *clips him round the ear.*

Rob Don't be asking a man about his money.

Luke You c-can't . . . bump into your . . . self.

Ben So . . . So hide away in a room somewhere, keep out of sight –

Luke But you d-didn't . . . buy a ticket. Your other y-you . . . did.

Ben I'm me, I did buy the ticket. Aren't you complicating something very simple?

Luke Build your . . . ow-own v-v-then.

Rob He's not having a go, Luke. He's just – I mean, fucking hell. I don't understand it either. Just a quick nip back for a million quid.

Ben (*to* **Rob**) You haven't had a go, either?

Rob   He won't tell us how to work it.

Says if we fuck around with it, it'll tear us to pieces.

Luke   It's n-not . . . worth it.

Ben   It's not?

Luke   M-messing ar-around with all of . . . time and space.
Just for money.

Greg   All that butterfly stuff.

Ben   Butterfly effect.

Greg   Aye, that's what I meant.

Ben   But you haven't even gone back, experimented, things
like that?

Luke   Not worth it.

Ben   So you made a time machine just to let it sit in your
house? As a talking point?

Luke   I d-didn't . . . mean to make it. A-accident.

Ben   But you kept it.

Luke   W-well. You can't chuck a . . . time machine out.

He smiles to himself.

Beat.

Ben   What were you trying to make?

Greg   He won't tell anyone that, man –

Luke   I'm n-not –

Rob   Come on. Spill it, man.

Luke   C-can't.

Pause.

Ben *is still looking at the box.*

Ben   Why don't you sell it?

Luke *shakes his head.*

Ben   Why not?

Luke   C-can't let it g-get in the wro-wrong hands.

Ben   Sell it to someone you can trust.

Luke   Who?

Ben   I'll buy it.

Greg   Luke, he's loaded, him!

Rob (*smacking him*)   Shut up!

Beat.

Ben   I'll buy it.

Luke *shakes his head.*

Ben   You haven't seen how much I'm offering.

Luke *shakes his head.*

Pause.

Ben *fumbles in his pockets for a scrap of paper and a pen.*

He writes something down, then crosses the room and tries to give it to **Luke**, *who shakes his head again.* **Ben** *gently takes* **Luke**'s *hand and puts the paper in it.*

The Man *whimpers.*

Beat.

Ben   Take a look.

Luke *shakes his head.*

Rob   At least have a look, Luke. Jesus.

Beat.

Luke *looks quickly, then shakes his head.*

Greg   What's it say, Luke?

Ben   What if I double that?

Luke *shakes his head.*

Beat.

Ben   I'll triple it.

Greg   Fucking *hell*, man!

Luke   N-n . . . not for s-s . . . sale.

He scrumples the paper up and goes to the kitchen to put it in the bin.

Rob   Luke, come on.

Luke   N-no.

Rob   Can't you just make anoth –

Luke   *No.*

Beat.

He heads off to his room.

We hear a door shut.

Beat.

Greg   How much was it, Ben?

Rob   Just give him a bit of time, he might come round.

Ben   Well. We'll see.

Rob   There's only so long he can live like this. He'll be desperate for any money, soon.

Ben (*still looking at the box*)   Hm.

Pause.

Greg   How much was it, Ben?

Rob   Fucking shut up. None of your business.

Beat.

Ben *turns on his heels and heads to leave.*

Rob   You off?

Ben *nods.*

He takes a tenner out of his wallet and hands it to **Greg***.*

Ben   Clean upstairs. It's not locked.

He leaves, as quickly as that. **Greg** *calls after him.*

Greg   Wh – Yeah, man – No worries. I'll do a top job, too!

He shuts the door, beaming.

Tenner!

Rob   He's paying you to be his monkey boy.

Greg   You've got to start somewhere, don't you? Everyone starts with sweeping.

Mebbe soon I'll be working with yous proper!

Rob   Don't hold your breath.

Enter **Luke***.*

Greg   You wanna get in with Ben, man. He's *minted*. Just gave me a tenner.

He waves his tenner.

Rob   You're insulting him. He's offering you a fortune –

Greg   How much was it?

Luke   It doesn't . . . matter.

Rob   It doesn't matter? You don't think we could use the money?

Luke   No one can . . . have it.

Rob   Why? What's he gonna do?

Luke   Doing *a-anything* with it is dangerous. No one should – I should just . . . bin it.

Greg   Don't bin the time machine, man.

Rob   You could get out of this shit hole.

Luke   I'm fine –

Rob   He's trying to help us here – He's –

Luke   Money isn't g-going to . . . fix everything.

Rob   You can't build a time machine and not use it. That's an insult to, to, *science*.

Greg   You should at least give it a crack.

Luke *shakes his head and sits down on the sofa, fuming.*

Pause.

Greg   Do you know what I'd use it for?

Rob   No one cares.

Greg   Naw, but – Do you know –

Rob   No one gives a shite, man.

Greg   Just let us say it, though. (*Beat.*) I'd kill Hitler.

Beat.

Rob *and* **Luke** *laugh.*

Rob   You thick bastard.

Greg   What?

Rob   How are you gonna kill Hitler?

Greg   Cos I'll find out when he was, in like, back then, and go kill him when he's on the bog or sommit.

Rob   What about his guards?

Greg   He –

Luke   What about the p-police?

Greg   No one's gonna arrest me for killing Hitler, man. I'd be a hero.

Luke   So you'd kill him during the . . . w-war?

Greg   Naw . . . Naw, I'd kill him, before he could do any of the bad stuff he did.

Rob   So people won't know who he is.

Greg   Naw, they –

Luke   So you'll get ar-arrested.

Greg   No man, I'd –

Rob   You can't even talk back to the scrat ends on the street, how are you gonna *kill* someone?

Greg   Cos it's *Hitler*. Anyone could kill Hitler.

Rob   You couldn't.

Greg   I could! Specially if he was sat taking a dump.

Luke   I think he'd be pr-pretty well protected.

Greg   Not on the – It's not – Fucking bollocks to you. I was just saying.

Rob   Well, don't next time.

Greg (*heading for the door*)   I can't stay round here anyways. I've got things to do for Ben.

Rob   Yeah, sweeping his empty flat. He's given you the keys to the fucking kingdom there.

Luke *laughs.*

Greg   Always taking the piss –

Ben's gonna help us *make* something of myself, so yous can both fuck off!

Greg *slams the door behind him.*

Rob   He's funny, that one.

Pause.

Rob *fishes in his pocket for a biscuit, which he feeds to* **The Man**.

Rob   So we should – Stop slobbering on my hand, you daft cunt –

We should talk about this flat, then.

Luke   What?

Rob   Well, you can't be staying round here, can you?

Luke   I'm staying.

Rob   You can't afford it though, can you?

Luke   The c-council –

Rob   Aye, the council are paying the rent, but what about your food and that?

Luke   I –

Rob   I can't keep paying you an allowance like this, can I? Specially since you don't agree with where my money's coming from.

Beat.

Luke   You . . . don't have to.

Rob   I'll just cut you off then, yeah?

Luke *nods.*

Rob   You're alright without me?

Luke *nods.*

Rob   You're independent.

Beat.

You'll get a job then, eh?

Luke   M-maybe.

Rob   Definitely. You've got bills to pay.

Luke   I can . . . get one.

Rob   Well, probably get some pub work or sommit maybe. Work in a takeaway. Without GCSEs people might not give a fuck anywhere else.

Luke   D-don't –

Rob   Probably should have seen them through, yeah?

Luke   Y –

Rob   And to be honest mate, I don't know what pub or takeaway wants an employee who can't string his sentences together.

Pause.

This is just another fuck-up in your long line of fuck-ups, eh? Someone offers you qualifications, you turn them down. Someone offers you enough money to be set –

Luke   You don't . . . understand.

He gets up as if to do something, but doesn't have anything to do.

Rob   Oh yeah, it's complicated. Too much for me to understand. You've got a talent for making – fucking, fucking *time machines*! And then they just sit in your shit flat. Why even make it in the first fucking place?

Luke   It's not about . . . that.

Rob   Even Specky Cunt gets it – Even he knows to take what he can get –

Luke   I d-don't –

Rob   But every chance you've had, every opportunity you've been given, you've ignored.

I spend my life working to, to, *feed* you –

Luke   It's not –

Rob   – and you're sitting on your arse like you've got everything you could ever want from life –

Luke   I'll g-get a *job*.

Rob   Good. Cos I'm finished making sacrifices for you.

Luke   I didn't *ask* you to . . . m-make –

Rob   Course you didn't *ask* me! I was making them before you could fucking *walk*!

Pause.

The Man *whimpers and lies down.*

Luke   Just look after your . . . self.

Rob   What's your job? Eh? What are you doing?

Luke   Well I haven't . . . g –

Rob   What? Where are you gonna work?

Pause.

Luke *mumbles.*

Rob   You what?

Luke   N . . . Nasa. I'm gonna work for Nasa.

Beat.

Rob   *Nasa?*

Luke *nods.*

Rob   Fucking *Nasa?*

Luke   So?

Rob   You can't work for Nasa.

Luke   Why not?

Rob   People from round here don't go and work at Nasa. It's in America, for fuck's sake.

Luke   I can b-build a time . . . machine, I think they'll be i-interested in us.

Pause.

Rob   Right. Good. Give em a bell then.

Luke   Wh –

Rob *tosses his phone at* **Luke**, *who catches it awkwardly.*

Rob   Give em a ring. Get yourself an interview.

Luke   You . . . can't just –

Rob   You want a job at Nasa, make the fucking effort.

Luke   I don't know . . . who –

Rob   Ring 118.

Beat.

Luke *dials 118 118.*

Pause.

Luke   It's r-r –

Someone picks up.

Luke (*into phone*)   Oh- . . . I . . . I . . . I . . . Y . . . Y . . . Y . . .

Rob   Fuck's *sake.*

He goes and snatches the phone.

(*Into phone.*) Can I have the number for Nasa please . . . In America . . . Yeah . . . I *know*, just give us the number . . . It's *Nasa*, I think you can find the number . . .

(*To* **Luke**.) She's getting it.

Pause.

Rob *shakes his head.*

Rob   Nasa . . .

Beat.

(*Into phone.*) Alright . . . Cheers . . . (*To* **Luke**.) She's putting us through now.

Pause.

Rob   It's ringing. (*Beat.*) Think of sommit to say.

Luke   Wh –

Rob   Think of good stuff to say, why they should hire you and that.

Luke   I don't –

Rob   Fucking – ! Hang on –

He hangs up quickly.

How much is that gonna cost me, calling Nasa?

Luke   I d-didn't . . . ask you to.

Rob   Course you didn't. You'd never do anything if I didn't bully you into it.

Luke   Stop playing the . . . m-martyr.

Rob   What's that?

Luke   L-like a saint.

Rob   I am a fucking saint!

Luke *heads off down the corridor.* **Rob** *calls after him.*

Rob   Do you think I want to spend my days walking round these estates?

Dealing with these fucking smack-rats? Why do you think I do it?

Luke (*off*)   You e-enjoy it.

Rob   Do I fuck!

Luke (*off*)   You like the power.

He appears in the doorway.

Y-you like being the . . . big man.

Rob   Fuck off.

Luke   Like having a reputation as a mad . . . bastard.

Rob   I'm doing this for *you*. We're a *family*.

Luke   You wrecked our family.

Pause.

I mean –

Rob   What do you remember? About when you were little?

Beat.

Luke   Wh –

Rob   Do you know what I remember?

I remember waiting outside pubs with you in your pram, waiting for Dad to get thrown out and battered, so we could go home.

Playing fucking . . . stupid games and that. That's what I remember.

I remember walking you to school every day.

Luke   I'm n-not having a . . . go about that.

Rob   Least you *got* a fucking childhood.

Luke   W-wait –

Rob   I *am* your family.

Have a think and tell me how often Dad appears in your version of things.

Cos he fucked off pretty fucking sharpish –

Luke   Is it better now you're keeping him on a . . . lead?

Pause.

Rob   Least I know where he is.

The Man *has been moving strangely throughout this and now starts to whimper.*

Rob *goes over to him.*

Rob   Climbing the walls here. Let him kip here after his fix.

Luke   Wh . . . I d-don't –

Rob   Just let him kip here on the floor, alright? Not too much to ask, is it? He's not gonna do owt but sleep.

During the following **Rob** *takes a little wrap out of his pocket and gives it to* **The Man**, *who opens his bumbag and takes his works out.*

He shoots up quietly, **Rob** *helping him with the first fiddly stages.*

After he's injected into his thigh, he curls up and goes to sleep.

Rob *stands up and looks at his phone.*

Luke (*watching* **The Man**)   He's . . . just gonna sleep?

Rob   Just leave him be. He won't bother you. Go write your CV. / Send Nasa a letter.

Luke   Rob, man –

Rob   I'll be back for him later.

Rob *exits, his phone to his ear.*

Pause.

Luke *looks at* **The Man**, *who is almost asleep.*

Luke (*quietly*)   Fucking . . . idiot.

Fade.

Three

The same, late that night.

The Man *is awake and sitting up in the corner.*

He looks around the room and fiddles with his scarf.

Luke *is asleep on his mattress on the floor.*

Pause.

There's a knock at the door.

Pause.

There's a knock at the door.

Luke *stirs.*

He looks over to **The Man**, *who whimpers.*

He sits up, rubbing his eyes.

There's a knock at the door.

Luke   Finally c-come back for you.

He gets up and goes over to the door. He turns the light on, squinting.

He opens the door.

It's **Ben**.

Luke   O . . . Oh. I f-f . . .

Ben   You thought it was your brother?

Luke *nods.*

Beat.

Ben   Can I come in?

Beat.

Luke   I'm n-n . . .

Ben   You shouldn't just open your door at this time.

Luke   I kn –

Ben   Could have been anyone.

Luke   Y –

Ben   You should get one of those little spyholes. For the door.

Beat.

Rob said he was stopping by. Can I wait?

Beat.

It won't be long.

Luke *gestures* **Ben** *in, reluctantly.*

He shuts the door.

Ben *sits on the sofa.*

Beat.

Ben   Sorry for waking you.

Luke   Th-that's –

Ben   I know it's late, but your brother said to meet him here.

He smiles at **Luke**.

Beat.

Luke *sits down at the table.*

He feeds his fish.

Ben *looks at* **The Man**.

Ben   Are you dog-sitting?

He smiles.

Pause.

Why do you sleep in here?

Luke   Hm?

Ben   Why do you sleep in here?

Luke   I, I . . . use the b-bedroom to w-w –

Ben   To work in.

Luke *nods.*

Ben   It's your lab. The bedroom.

Luke *nods.*

Ben   Can I see it?

Luke   S-s-sorry.

Beat.

Ben   Why don't you just work in here?

Luke   Th-th-there's no . . . window in the bedroom.

Ben   So no one can see in?

Luke *nods.*

Ben   Because you don't want people to steal your ideas.

Luke *nods.*

Beat.

Ben *nods to himself.*

He gets up and starts walking around the room.

He looks out of the window, looks in the kitchen, etc.

Ben   How long have you been here now?

Luke   N-not . . . long. A couple of muh-muh –

Ben   Couple of months. Do you like it?

Luke *shrugs.*

Ben   You were living with Rob before.

Luke *nods.*

Ben   But you're glad to be out.

Luke *nods*.

Ben   Got your independence. How old are you now?

Luke   Uh, nye-nye −

Ben   Nineteen. (*Nods*.) I remember nineteen. Good year.

Luke *shrugs*.

Ben   Seemed to fuck a lot of girls at nineteen. Have you had a lot of attention?

From girls?

Beat.

Luke *shrugs*.

Ben   Are you still a virgin?

Beat.

Luke   Wh-wh − ?

Ben   It's alright. Just making conversation.

Pause.

Rob's told me a lot about you.

And Greg, too. Neither of them can shut up about you.

They're big talkers. Sort of the opposite to you, I guess.

How long have you had that . . . your voice?

Luke *shrugs*.

Ben   Long time?

Luke   Y-y −

Ben   You had it at school?

Luke *nods*.

Ben   Did people think you were stupid?

Beat.

Did they make fun of you?

Luke   A . . . bit.

Ben (*nods*)   People think that. If you can't articulate yourself. They think you're stupid. Like people who don't speak English. People always end up patronising people like that. I bet you get patronised a lot. Do you?

Luke *shrugs.*

Ben   Happens with accents, too. People with, slightly more . . . well *rounded* accents. Tend to be thought of as more intelligent. Even if they're not.

Beat.

Interesting though. People's expectations. You can use them to your advantage. Like you have. You think perhaps you worked harder to prove people wrong?

Luke *shrugs.*

Ben   People expect you to be stupid so you prove them wrong.

But then, people expected you to pass your exams, didn't they?

What happened there?

Beat.

Luke   I just . . . didn't see . . . the point.

Ben   You could've gone to university.

Luke   D-don't . . . care. I can . . . read.

Ben   It's not about that though. Course you can read, it's not about that.

It's about the social aspect.

Luke   I'm not really . . . interested in p-people.

Ben   You don't like people so much?

Luke *shakes head.*

Ben   Why's that?

Beat.

Luke   They . . . let you down. They're . . . selfish. Can't r-rely on them.

Ben   What about your brother? You can't rely on him?

Luke *shakes head.*

Ben   Do you trust your brother?

Luke *shakes head.*

Ben   You don't?

Luke *shakes head.*

Ben   Why not?

Luke   . . . he's a . . . cr-criminal.

Ben   And that means you can't trust him?

Luke *shrugs.*

Ben   He practically *raised* you, didn't he?

Luke   He's . . . fucked up a lot . . . too.

Ben   Well, it must have been hard.

Doing that alone.

Pause.

You don't like me very much, do you?

Beat.

Luke   I . . . just don't . . . know y-you.

Beat.

That's . . . all.

Ben   I can understand it. Turning up out the blue and throwing money around.

Luke   Wh-why *have* you . . . come here?

Ben   To meet Rob.

Luke   N-no . . . to B-B –

Ben   To Boro? To work.

Luke   Why . . . not just w-work in . . . London?

Ben   All sorts of reasons. Money reasons.

Luke   Why did you . . . p-pick Rob?

Ben   Will that make you feel better? If I explain myself?

Luke   Maybe.

Pause.

Ben   I like Middlesbrough. That's one reason.

Luke   Wh-*why?*

Ben   Because. It's interesting. It's falling to pieces. Some parts –

Round here.

Looks like you've had a war no one noticed.

All these green grilles on the windows and doors . . .

Feels like the, the *Wild West*, or something.

. . .

Have you seen the kid . . . There's a boy driving round on a quadbike.

He just drives round and round the block all day.

Luke   He's an . . . idiot.

Ben   I talked to him yesterday. His shoes are held together with tape.

He's got a quadbike but he doesn't have shoes.

You think if he had the drive to steal a quadbike, he'd pinch a pair of shoes too.

I said I'd give him ten pounds if he went and punched this lad on the other side of the street. Big lad.

He can't have been half the size of him, but straight away he rode his quadbike over and started pummelling him in the head. Eventually the other lad fought back and beat him half to death. But he still limped back over, pushing his bike, asking for his tenner.

I hadn't even *shown* him the money.

That's – You can see the potential there.

In a microcosm.

That kind of thing, you can expand that to include whole estates. A whole town.

Beat.

Luke   Y-you c-can't . . . *buy* a town.

Ben   No. You can't. But you can make people think you can. If they're weak enough.

Luke   You're . . . Sc-Scarface, then?

Ben (*smiles*)   Nothing as glamorous as that. Just common sense.

Anyone can buy the more desperate people on the bottom, the people without options.

Like your friend.

Then once you've got enough of those people – and there's a lot of them around in Middlesbrough – you can just keep going. And going.

As long as you've got the biggest wallet –

Then suddenly you're the biggest employer.

It doesn't work in London because there's too many – It's too big. Too much for one person.

But round here, it's a small enough pen. And everyone in it is bored and angry.

And mostly unemployed.

All you have to do is control the three pastimes. Drugs, prostitution, then eventually alcohol; once you start taking control of the pubs, then –

Luke   R-Rob's . . . not into that.

Ben   He's into money. He's into improving his situation.

And yours.

Luke   He's not i-interested in . . . the rest.

Ben (*smiles*)   No. He's got narrow horizons. Keeps talking about 'putting money back'. Community centres, playgrounds.

Luke   Y-you don't . . . care about that.

Ben   It's not that I don't care, Luke. It's . . . it's that it's pointless.

Have you looked out your window? How many houses on this street are boarded up? Half of them? Three-quarters? Anyone with an ounce of sense has moved away. The rest just stay inside. There's nothing out there but bored kids and waste.

I mean, for Christ's sake, your brother keeps a demented junkie on a *dog lead*. And no one cares! No one.

You can't fix that with a playground or a community centre.

They'll just be meeting points for more of the same.

So why shouldn't we exploit the market that's left? Turn it into something productive.

Beat.

Luke   S-sounds . . . horrible. Sounds like . . . a film or something . . . Bad film.

Ben (*smiles*)   Maybe. But I don't see how it won't be an improvement.

Greg seems to agree.

I think he's felt a bit undervalued in the past. But now he has a *purpose* . . .

Luke   Being your b-butler?

Ben   I'm giving people options.

And there haven't been many options round here for a while.

None that I can see, anyway.

Pause.

Why are you so desperate to stay?

Luke   I'm . . . fine.

Ben   You're so much better than the rest of them.

Luke   I'm n-n –

Ben   Look at him –

He goes over to **The Man**.

Is he ever going to cure cancer?

Or discover the new world?

Explore space?

Of course not.

But you might.

He's here to fail so the rest of us –

Luke   Leave him.

Pause.

Ben   Surely given the chance, you'd be somewhere else?
Somewhere with less blood in the gutters.

He is now by the box.

Beat.

There's some houses I've been looking at in Marton.

It's a nice area, not too far away.

I'll buy one for you and your brother. Give you a lump sum –

Luke   I d-d-don't want to live . . . with Rob.

Ben   Just you then.

Luke   You can't have it.

Beat.

You can't have the box. N-n-no one can.

Beat.

I don't care . . . how rich you are.

I d-don't care if you've . . . got Greg running round a-after you.

You c-can't buy a . . . whole town.

And you can't buy . . . me.

Beat.

Ben   What about your brother?

Luke   Wh, wh –

Ben   Don't you think he'd like a new start?

Luke   He's, he's –

Ben   I think he'd appreciate some stability.

Luke   You're, you're helping –

Ben   Only for now.

I have to start at the bottom.

That just happens to be where Rob operates.

Beat.

There are *hundreds* of Robs. There's only one of these. You –

Luke   You can't *have* it.

You can't. I d-don't care what you say.

You *can't*. I won't s-sell it for . . . me or . . . Rob. N-none of you understand it.

None of you.

You're all . . . f-fucking *stupid*.

. . .

You th-think you're better than everyone here. Just . . . cos you have money.

W-well, I don't *care* about that. And j-just cos you can make people round here . . . do things for you by p-paying em, doesn't mean you . . . *own* them.

Ben   If you say so.

Luke   I . . . *do*. I do . . . say so. And Rob'll . . . suss you out soon enough. He'll w-work out who you . . . are. He's just . . . impressed with you now. But that'll . . . wear off.

Pause.

Ben *goes over to* **Luke***, who backs away instinctively.*

He takes **The Man***'s lead.*

Ben   Sorry for waking you. I'll wait upstairs.

He heads out the door, dragging **The Man***.*

Luke   H-hey – You sh-shouldn't –

Ben *shuts the door behind him.*

A silence.

Luke *listens as a door upstairs slams. There is a muffled voice.*
Some bumps and footsteps. Strange noises.

A silence.

The intercom buzzes.

Luke *jumps.*

Beat.

He answers it.

Luke   H –

Intercom   It's me.

He presses the button and opens the door.

Enter **Rob**.

Rob   Soz I'm so late – Where's he –

Luke   B-Ben has him. Upstairs.

Rob   *Ben* has him?

Luke   R-Rob, he's mental.

Rob   He's –

Luke   He's properly mental –

He shuts the door. He keeps glancing at the ceiling, worried **Ben** *can hear.*

Luke   He, he . . . wants to, like – He, he, he –

Rob   Calm down.

Beat.

Luke   He th-thinks he can *buy* everything. He . . . says he's going to buy all of . . . Boro.

Rob   What?

Luke   He wants to b-be some sort of . . . *king*. He's *mental*.

Rob   He's just got a lot of cash. He's talking, like, hypothetical.

Luke   He's . . . *cr-crazy*.

Pause.

Rob   You need to make more of an effort with him.

Luke   Rob –

Rob   He's our chance at something better, alright? You don't even want to *know* how wadded he is. It's ridiculous. And he doesn't *care*. He just throws it around.

Luke   He's a *psy-sycho*.

Rob   Pack it in! (*Beat.*) He's putting faith in me, alright? Do you think I'm the only one round here – Do you think I'm like, a, a, *specialist* or something? The only reason I don't get fucked with is because I work small scale and I've fucking . . . glassed enough people to keep em away. That doesn't last, alright? (*Beat.*) We *need* him. Who knows, maybe he'll, he'll, buy us a *house* or something. But just cos you've fallen out over your magic box –

Luke   He's *obsessed* with it –

Rob   I don't care, man –

Luke   This isn't –

Rob   If I wasn't doing this, there'd be no long-term plan, alright?

Beat.

I don't have a pension. I don't have any guarantees that we can keep eating.

I want better for us.

Luke   *Please*, you've got to –

Rob   No. (*Beat.*) Grow up, alright?

He huffs his inhaler.

Go back to bed.

Exit **Rob**.

Pause.

Luke *turns the light off.*

Beat.

He stares at the ceiling and listens to the footsteps and muffled voices upstairs.

He looks over to the box.

Fade.

Spacemen

While the house lights are still up, **The Man** *wanders on to the stage.*

He looks younger, clean, and is dressed smartly in a shirt and jeans.

As he speaks, the house lights go down, and **The Man** *is lit with a pale wash.*

He lights a cigarette.

He holds up his right hand.

The Man   You can see –

He wiggles the fingers.

I dunno if you can see –

I broke two of these fingers here –

I bet –

He asks someone sat on the front row. Use answers as appropriate.

Can you tell which ones – Sorry love (*or mate*), blowing smoke in your face.

Can you tell which ones?

Beat.

He wiggles them.

Aye, those ones. The middle two.

Or –

No, the middle ones, there. You can see, when I wiggle them.

He goes back to addressing the whole audience. He's very casual.

The middle two, here.

I broke them a good couple of years ago now, but they've never been the same.

They work alright and everything. Get the job done.

But they're a bit – not, not stiff, but – *different*.

Just feel a bit different. Specially when it's cold.

They don't even feel like my fingers when it's cold.

I dunno whether that's normal. To feel like your fingers aren't your fingers.

He wiggles them.

I broke em when I was –

It's daft. That's why I bring it up, to tell you about this daft . . .

Our Robert –

That's my eldest.

He's –

This is a few years ago now, when he was . . . maybe nine. About nine. And Luke was barely talking at two. Not that he did much talking to be honest, he's never been much of a talker.

Robert's about nine. And he's always been a bit young for his age.

He's not ever had many friends that he hangs around with, prefers to be mucking about on his own in the yard and whatever.

He's got his –

We've got this little shed. Out in the back.

We don't use it for anything, it's from whoever had the house before us. It's all full of junk, you know. Full of crap.

Not even car-boot fodder, just crap. Bike wheels without tyres and broken chairs and things like that. No one goes in there.

No one cept Robert, anyway.

Right from when he could walk he's been obsessed with this shed.

Think he's convinced if he keeps looking through all the shite in there, he might find a bag of gold coins or a new bike, or sommit.

I kept telling him to stay out of it – it's full of broken glass and rusty nails – but after a while it got to the point where he was sneaking in there any minute I wasn't looking, so I just let him get on with it.

I did say he had to wear his goalie gloves, mind. To be a bit of protection against tetanus and all that. Course, he doesn't know what tetanus is. Not that I can really explain it either; but we both know it's bad, and I was just pleased his goalie gloves were getting some use at least.

Begged me for goalie gloves. Absolutely *begged* me. Day and night.

In the end I pinched a pair from the Hill Street and told him he'd better be putting them to use. Course, he wore them round the house for a week non-stop, ate his frigging tea in them and everything, but I don't think they ever touched a football.

Anyway.

He's turned this shed full of junk into his den, and he sits in there and that.

Luke's not allowed in there, but I catch him trying to crawl in enough times. Inseparable, the pair of em, so I have to put down another rule and say, Robert, you make sure Luke doesn't go in any further than that doorway.

And he's pretty good at keeping to that, to be fair to him.

I still keep an eye, out the kitchen window, but they're both good at sticking to the rule.

Luke's content to just sit there and read his Hungry
Caterpillar for the hundredth time. Or my paper. He likes my
paper. He can't read it yet, course. But he wraps it round
himself like a little suit, you know?

He laughs a little.

Anyway, he's fine doing that, sitting in the doorway. Long as
they're close to each other, they're alright. They look out for
each other.

So one day it's just the usual, me sat in the kitchen, lads out in
the yard.

Robert was in the shed for a bit, but now he's running round
the yard shouting and that, playing some game with himself.
Luke sat there wearing my paper, all regal.

Then after a bit I hear some crying, and Robert calling for me,
voice all wobbly.

I go out, and he's got this fucking great fish bowl stuck on his
head. It's absolutely filthy, you can barely see his face through
it. He's staggering about and trying to yank it off his head, still
wearing his goalie gloves.

What have I told you about messing around in that shed?

'I can't get it off Dad . . . '

I say – I can see that. What are you doing sticking goldfish
bowls on your head in the first place?

'I was being a spaceman . . . '

He's crying more now, very upset.

Calm down, come on. Pack it in with that.

He says – 'I can't breathe though.'

Course you can breathe, if you can talk you can breathe.
You're talking, aren't you?

'Yeah . . . '

Then you're alright then.

He steadies out a bit.

I say – Now hang on a minute.

I go inside and get the marge out the fridge.

I say – I'm going to stick this round your head to make you all slippy, alright? Then it'll slide right off you.

He says – 'I don't like butter . . . '

It's not butter, it's marge.

'I don't like marge . . . '

I say – Well you don't have to eat it, do you?

I slop it round his chin and the bowl, getting it all slippy.

I'm gonna give it a yank now, alright?

'No, Dad! No, Dad!'

What?

'It's gonna break and get glass in my eyes!'

No it isn't.

'It is!'

It isn't!

'Is, Dad! It's gonna break!'

I say – Alright, alright. Hang on. Look. I'll –

He sticks his cigarette in his mouth so he's got both hands free.

He mimes holding the bowl with his left hand, and sliding his right hand up inside it.

There's just enough room for me to slide my hand in, when it's hanging round his neck. I've not got big hands. Never did.

I say – Right, there we are. Got my hand there protecting your face, alright?

'Will it be safe?'

It'll be fine. Any glass breaks it'll be my hand getting chopped to bits, alright?

He gives the sad nod of a scared nine-year-old.

Right then. Shut your eyes. One . . . two . . . three –

He mimes working the bowl off his son's head.

It's stuck on tight, but there's just enough wiggle room to work it off.

It starts coming off alright at first – though he's moaning a bit and his cheeks are all squashed up – but then we get to about the top of his nose and it gets much tighter.

I keep my hand on his face, keeping him safe.

He's moaning and my knuckles are getting crushed to fuck, but I say – It's alright, nearly there.

We get up to his eyes and I think right, one sharp tug and we're away.

So I give it a tug, and it starts coming well enough, but my fingers have slipped down so the bowl's right on my joints, and as I give it a last yank – which pulls his eyebrows up so he looks all surprised – there's a crunch and a yell – which is me –and my two middle fingers break just as quick as it slips off his head.

We both sit looking at this bowl, him wiping his nose and rubbing his face, me laughing.

Luke just looking at us like we're a right pair of dickheads.

Which we are.

It takes a bit to even realise that I've broken em. I'm just laughing and patting him on the head, suddenly finding everything hilarious.

I sit looking at how filthy this fish bowl is, and wondering what he was thinking sticking it on his head.

But that's the thing about Robert, you see. He's a good lad, and he's full of beans, but he doesn't think. He just runs around sticking his head places he shouldn't, getting into scrapes. Luckily, Luke's turned out to be the clever one, so hopefully he'll be able to keep an eye on him. Cos otherwise he's gonna end up with his head stuck somewhere worse than a fish bowl.

But that's how they work really, the two of em. They're a good team.

Luke's the thinker, and Robert's the doer. Luke barely opens his mouth unless he has to, but when he does speak, Robert's always listening carefully as he can, just in case it's a bit of information he's gonna need on his travels.

And I'm not saying Robert's thick or anything, he's not at all. Just, Luke's a lot more into his schoolwork and that, and Robert's more interested in his adventures.

And that's what I reckon they'll be up to when they're older.

Robert'll be the spaceman.

And Luke'll send him up there.

He smiles.

Crossfade.

Act Two

One

The same.

Evening.

Luke *is standing in the middle of the room. He looks around, confused.*

He checks himself.

He nods.

He sits down.

Beat.

He stands up.

He looks at his watch, nervous.

Beat.

Luke   . . . H-hello?

Ben *enters from the bedroom.*

Luke   N-n-n-n,n,n,n / n,n,n,n −

Ben   It's alright Luke, calm down. Calm down.

He grabs one of the chairs and puts it down in the middle of the room.

Have a sit-down.

Beat.

Come on, sit down. Let's chat.

Luke *sits down.*

Pause.

Ben   Have you had a think since last night?

Luke *nods.*

Ben   And you feel the same?

Luke *nods.*

Beat.

Ben   Do you know what I'm going to do to you?

Luke *nods.*

Ben   You do?

Luke *nods.*

Beat.

Ben   How can you when I haven't done it yet?

. . . You don't know everything.

Pause.

Let me get you a glass of water.

He leaves to the kitchen.

The tap runs.

Luke *looks at his watch, then at the door.*

Ben *returns with a glass of water and hands it to* **Luke***.*

Ben   Have a bit, Luke. Have a sip.

Beat.

Luke *drinks shakily.*

Beat.

Ben   I've just had a look in your lab. (*Beat.*) What are you up to in there?

Beat.

Luke   I – I– I, I, I, I, I –

Ben   Alright, alright. It doesn't look like much anyway, if I'm honest.

Pause.

He crouches down in front of **Luke**.

Ben   I'm sorry it's come to this. I am.

Luke   / W, w, w, w –

Ben   But you weren't *listening*.

If you're not listening it's difficult to work things out any other way.

Pause.

Do you know what the three currencies are, Luke?

Beat.

Luke *shakes head.*

Ben   There are three ways, that society recognises, of getting what you want.

The first is money. The second is sex. And the third is violence.

Most things you can get the first way. I've gotten other things the second way, and since you won't take my money, I'll have to get what I want from you the third way.

Can you understand that?

Beat.

Luke *nods.*

Ben   I want you to know, that I don't want to do this.

I offered you money. I offered you a, a *house*.

I gave you plenty of options.

Luke   I, I, I, I –

Ben   So this isn't a personal gesture, I don't want you to take this personally.

But this is the choice you made.

He takes a pair of pliers out of his back pocket awkwardly, still crouched.

He remains casual and relaxed.

Now, I'll explain the rules to you. The first rule is, if you say *anything* to your brother, I mean, if you tell him I came round here, if you tell him I did what I'm going to do –

Then I will let the police know about the large amounts of various substances at his address. But not before I pay some friends to beat him until he can't digest food any more.

Alright? Let me know you're listening.

Luke *nods.*

Ben   The second rule is, is you have to be gone from here, from this flat, by tomorrow at six o'clock. I'm giving you plenty of time to move out. Okay?

Luke *nods.*

Ben   And the third rule is that you will leave me a clean, neatly written set of instructions for the box. These instructions will be clear and simple, and they'll cover everything I'd ever want to know about it. Okay?

If you mess me around – and I'll know if you have – I will hurt your brother, *and* you.

In a way that will drastically alter your lifestyle. Okay? Understand?

Luke *nods.*

Ben   Alright. Now. One last opportunity. A last chance.

Ben *takes the glass from* **Luke** *and puts it down.*

Ben   If you can say, ah, 'Please don't do this Ben' –

Without stuttering or stammering or any of that, I'll give you the old deal. The house, the money, and I won't tear your teeth out. There's no way for you to keep the flat, that's not going to happen. But you can improve your situation. Alright?

Luke *nods.*

Ben   Okay.

Pause.

Luke   . . . P-l-lease . . . d-don −

Ben   I'm sorry, Luke.

Luke   N-n-n, n, n −

Ben *stands up.*

Luke   Nnnn −

Ben *pulls* **Luke**'s *mouth open and presses a knee to his chest.*

Ben   I'll be as quick as I can, alright?

He pushes the pliers into **Luke**'s *mouth.*

Beat.

Ben *struggles to get a grip on a tooth.*

Ben   Just let me −

Beat.

He starts pulling on one of **Luke**'s *teeth.*

Luke *screams in agony, kicking his legs and trying to push him away.*

Ben *pulls harder, pushing* **Luke**'s *head away from him..*

Eventually the tooth tears out.

Luke *screams into* **Ben**'s *hand.*

Ben (*inspecting the tooth*)   It's alright, Luke. One's enough. One's enough.

He lets **Luke** *go, who clutches his face and cries quietly.*

Ben *takes* **Luke**'s *hand and drops the tooth in it.*

Ben   Now if you don't follow the rules, there'll be more, and then other body parts, and we don't want to get into it, alright? You remember the rules, don't you? Luke? The rules? Let me know you're listening.

Luke *nods weakly.*

Ben   Alright then. (*Beat.*) I'll leave you be.

Ben *heads to leave.*

Ben   Six o'clock, Luke.

I'm sorry.

He leaves, leaving the door open.

Pause.

Luke *takes his hand away from his mouth carefully. He whimpers.*

Blood is drooling out of his mouth.

He works his mouth a little, wincing.

He stands up, awkwardly.

He looks at his watch.

Luke 1 *appears in the doorway with a pizza box.*

He looks at the open door.

Luke 1   Wh what the f –

He sees **Luke 2**. *He steps into the flat.*

Pause.

Luke 1   / Wha, wha –

Luke 2   Jus-jus –

Luke 1   / Y, y, y, y –

Luke 2   Ha-hang, jus,

Pause.

Luke 1 Y-you're . . . ?

Luke 2 *nods.*

Pause.

Luke 1 *shuts the door.*

Beat.

Luke 1 (*he gestures to his face*)   What's –

Luke 2 Ben pulled my t-tooth out.

Luke 1 What?

Luke 2 Just now.

Luke 1 But –

Luke 2 I need –

Luke 1 Why's he pulling my teeth out?

Luke 2 Can you get us something . . . (*He gestures.*)

Luke 1 Soz, yeah, yeah.

Luke 1 *dumps his pizza box and goes to the kitchen.*

He comes back with a tea towel for **Luke 2**, *who puts it in his mouth.*

Pause.

Luke 1 *touches* **Luke 2**.

Luke 2 Gerroff.

Luke 1 Sorry.

Beat.

Luke 2 He says you have to be out of the flat by six tomorrow and leave him instructions for the box.

Luke 1 Right. Shit.

Luke 2 Or he'll, you know, do stuff. To us.

Luke 1 Did you know this was gonna happen?

Luke 2 (*nods*)   It's my second time.

Luke 1   Secon – Oh, right. Course.

Beat.

Does it hurt?

Luke 2   Course it hurts, he pulled my tooth out. Knacks.

Luke 1   Soz, yeah.

Luke 2   *Twice.* I could have let you take this one.

Beat.

Luke 1   When are you from?

Luke 2   Tomorrow.

Luke 1   Shouldn't be using it –

Luke 2   I know –

Luke 1   It's dangerous –

Luke 2   I *had* to. Don't you think if I'm here, something bad's happened?

I *had* to come back.

Something –

Rob and D-D-Dad . . .

Beat.

Luke 1   What?

Luke 2   I can't tell you.

Luke 1   Course.

Luke 2   But it's very bad. Extremely bad.

Luke 1   Okay.

Luke 2   And I'm here –

Luke 1   To change it. Right.

It's a lot to take in.

The toilet flushes offstage. The two turn to look down the corridor.

Enter **Greg***, doing his belt. He wears a ski mask.*

He looks at the two **Lukes***.*

Beat.

He makes a break for the door.

He manages to get just outside it when both **Lukes** *drag him back in.*

Greg   No! Nooo! Why's there two of yous?! Why's there two of yous?!

The **Lukes** *throw him whimpering onto the sofa.*

Luke 1 *interrogates him while* **Luke 2** *watches.*

Luke 1   What are you doing?

Greg   I'm not Greg.

Luke 1   Are you with Ben now?

Greg   Naw –

Luke 2   He is.

Greg   I am, but I wasn't –

Luke 1   Were you gonna help pull my tooth out?

Greg   Eh?

Luke 1 (*pointing at* **Luke 2***, who opens his mouth*)   Look at my mouth, man! Were you gonna help with that?

Greg   *No!*

Luke 2   You were s'posed to.

Greg   I didn't know he was gonna do that, honest, man! He said we just had to convince yous to move out. And then I went to the bog and he forgot about us.

I wasn't gonna pull anyone's teeth out, man! Promise!

Beat.

Luke 1 *relents.*

Luke 1   Fucking idiot.

Greg   Don't, man.

Luke 1   I always stuck up for you.

Greg   I didn't do owt –

Luke 1 (*yanking the ski mask off* **Greg**)   Working for that mentalist.

Greg   He forgot about us –

Luke 1   Anyone would forget about you.

Luke 1 *sits on the sofa.*

Greg *puts his glasses back on, which have been pulled off with the ski mask.*

Luke 2 *opens the pizza box and eats a slice slowly.*

Beat.

Greg   Why's there two of yous?

Luke 2   I'm from tomorrow.

Greg   Why, though?

Luke 2   I had to come back and help.

Greg   With what?

Luke 1   With something bad.

Greg   Don't you know what happens with everything?

Luke 1   He does, but he can't tell us.

Greg   Why?

Luke 1   Because.

Greg   Why, though?

Luke 1   Cos if he tells us then we'll do stuff different and it'll change everything and it could fuck up the whole world.

Greg   Can I have a bit of that?

Lukes   No you can't!

Beat.

Luke 1   What do I do now?

Luke 2   Nothing.

Luke 1   What did he say he'd do?

Luke 2   He'll hurt us.

All of us.

Luke 1 *paces.*

Greg   You should just give him the box, man.

Luke 2   Can't.

Greg   He'll leave yous alone if you do, though.

Luke 1   *Can't.*

Greg   What else can you do?

Luke 1 (*snapping*)   I'm not giving him the box, Greg.

Pause.

I'll have to break it.

Greg   Wh – Break it?

Luke 1   I can't let him get it. Is that what I'm supposed to – / Sorry.

Luke 2   Can't tell you.

Luke 1   But how could you get here / if – Sorry.

Luke 2   Can't tell you.

Beat.

Luke 1   That can't be what I do. Cos you're here.

Greg   He can't tell you, man.

Luke 1 *looks at his box.*

Pause.

I'm not breaking it just so he can't have it.

I'm not doing that. Why should I? It's mine. I worked for ages on it.

Greg   But he'll batter you and Rob –

Luke 1   He's not having it. He can't just have whatever he wants. Just cos he's got money and no one else does, doesn't mean he's the fucking king.

Greg   But Luke –

Luke 1   Fucking shut up, Greg!

Greg   I'm just saying, though –

Luke 1   Just cos he's your boss now. Just cos he *bought* you.

Greg   He didn't buy us –

Luke 1   He didn't? What are you doing wearing a ski mask then?

Greg   I'm not – You don't –

He springs up.

What have you ever done for us?

Luke 1   What?

Greg   Why should I look out for you? You never look out for me.

Luke 1   We're the only ones who ever did *anything* for you.

Greg   That's not – You don't get to treat us like a dickhead just cos I don't have any other friends. Ben gave me a job, and, *and* some money. He's giving me a chance – That's more than yous cunts ever did for us.

Luke 1   He's a fucking psychopath –

Greg   He gave you a choice!

. . .

I'm not going to miss out like you did –

I never had any chances from anyone, so you can fuck off if you think I owe you and Rob *anything*. Fuck off the pair of yous!

He rushes out of the door, slamming it behind him.

Beat.

Luke 2   That didn't happen last time.

Blackout.

Two

The same, the following day.

Late morning.

Luke 1 *is asleep on the sofa.* **Luke 2** *is on the mattress.*

The Man *sits watching them sleep.*

He rubs his eyes.

He rubs his scarf on his face.

He wanders over to **Luke 2** *and sits looking down at him.*

Luke 2 *slowly begins to wake up.*

He sees **The Man** *looking at him.*

A moment.

He reaches out and puts a hand on **The Man**'s *head.*

Beat.

Rob *comes in from the corridor.*

Rob (*quietly*)   Oi, you. Leave him alone.

The Man *leaves* **Luke 2** *and goes to sit in a corner.*

Rob *speaks quietly throughout.*

Rob   Your door was open. Not like you. (*Beat.*) You want some breakfast?

Luke 2 *nods.*

Rob   Got us a box of Coco Pops.

He goes and busies himself in the kitchen.

Luke 2 *gets up and wanders over to sit down at the table.*

He sneaks a look at **Rob** *through the serving hatch.*

Rob *comes out of the kitchen with two bowls of Coco Pops.*

He sloshes a bit of milk down his front.

Rob (*hissing*)   Fuck . . .

He puts the bowls down and brushes his front.

He's about to sit down when he remembers something and goes back into the kitchen.

He comes back with the box and puts it in between them.

Rob   Always read the box, didn't you?

Luke 2 *smiles, nods.*

They eat their breakfast.

Luke 2 *occasionally looks at* **Rob**.

A silence.

Rob   Fucking rubbish really, aren't they, Coco Pops? They go on about turning the milk chocolatey, but you don't get both like in the adverts.

Just soggy Rice Krispies in brown milk.

Pause.

He nods at the sofa.

Has he moved in now or something?

Luke 2 *shakes head.*

Rob   Seems like it. Mind you, I wouldn't want to live with his dad either.

Beat.

You alright?

Luke 2 *nods.*

Rob   Looking at us weird.

Luke 2 *shrugs.*

Rob   You mute as well as daft?

Luke 2 *shrugs.*

Rob   What were you doing last night?

Beat.

Luke 2   Not much.

Rob *notices* **Luke 2***'s face is a bit swollen.*

Rob   What's – Sommit wrong with your face?

Luke 2 *touches his cheek.*

Rob   Swelled up.

Luke 2   Bit my cheek.

Rob   Aw right. Knacks that.

A silence.

Luke, man –

He adjusts his hat nervously.

Rob   – I'm sorry we've been arguing and that . . .

Luke 2 *stares into his cereal.* **Rob** *looks anywhere around the room but at his brother.*

Rob   I've been a bit of a dick, like. (*Beat.*) And – And, I know, that, you know, uh, what I do –

My job.

It's fucking shit. And you hate it. And I admit, that, you know, I get satisfaction – But just cos I'm good at it. Just cos –Not for any sick reason or owt . . .

But,

I do wish –

That I could change some of the stuff. That I've done.

And –

I'm gonna –

I think I'll knock it on the head soon.

My job.

Couple of months, or sommit.

With Ben and that I should be able . . .

And I know he's a bit . . .

Different.

But I think he can help us to –

Save up a bit and everything.

Cos, like . . .

Cos . . .

Cos I don't wanna . . .

He readjusts his hat. He picks at the table.

. . . I don't wanna not see you and that. Cos of my job.

Cos I know you don't wanna be around all of it.

So mebbes, I dunno –

We could mebbes save up and get like a, a, rent a house in a nicer bit. If you want. With more rooms. So you can do your work, and I'll look after him (**The Man**), and I'll be nicer to him (**Greg**), and I won't bother you or owt, I'll let you get on with whatever you wanna be doing.

I just have to . . . keep us all together.

I know I've – fucked up a lot.

And if I could do it all again I don't know if I'd . . .

Pause.

He stands up and clears the bowls away.

Anyway. Soz. For fighting and that.

He rinses the dishes in the kitchen.

Luke 2 *looks shell-shocked.*

The Man *has been listening to all of this intently.*

Rob (*from kitchen*)   Is that alright though, yeah?

Luke 2   Y-yeah. Ch . . . cheers.

Rob (*from kitchen*)   Alright.

Luke 1 *is waking up.*

Rob *comes back out of the kitchen.*

Rob   So what are you doin –

He sees **Luke 1**.

He looks at **Luke 2**.

Beat.

Rob   What have you done now?!

Luke 1   It's, it's, alright, he's from t-tomorrow.

Rob   Eh?

Luke 2   I'm from . . . tomorrow – I . . . came back in the b-box.

Rob   What?

Luke 1   He's from –

The Man *looks worried.*

Rob   You're freaking him out. Go and stand outside.

Lukes   What?

Rob   One of you go and stand outside, you're freaking him out.

Luke 1   But –

Luke 2   I'll go, it's, it's, alright.

He leaves the flat, pulling the door behind him.

Rob (*to* **The Man**)   You're alright, calm down.

Beat.

Rob *gives* **Luke 1** *a look.*

Luke 1   What?

Rob   What? What the fuck do you think what?

Luke 1   H-he's me. From t-tomorrow.

Rob   From tomorrow.

Luke 1   He says we n-need him.

Rob   We need him.

Luke 1   He can't say . . . exact . . . ly why.

Rob   Why not?

Luke 1   If we know what's gonna h-happen it might . . . ruin everything.

Rob   Like how?

Luke 1   I dun-dunno. But it won't be . . . good.

Rob   You said no one should ever use –

Luke 1   Exactly. So it m-must be . . . important.

Beat.

S-something bad's gonna h-happen.

Beat.

Rob   I just sat talking to him.

Luke 1   It doesn't matter.

Beat.

Rob   I said a load of . . .

Beat.

Luke 1   He's, he's, still me.

Rob   You're you.

Luke 1 He is . . . too. It doesn't make m-much difference who you t-talk to. All of what h-happens to him will happen to me soon too.

Rob What?

Luke 1 C-cos I'll have to come back from tomorrow too . . . tomorrow.

When I . . . get to tomorrow.

Pause.

Rob Well this is a fucking mess, isn't it?

Luke 2 (*from outside*) Can I c-come back in yet?

Rob No you can't. What's wrong with his face?

Luke 1 Wh . . . ?

Rob His face is all swelled up.

Beat.

What?

Luke 1 (*calling*) L-Luke –

Luke 2 (*from outside*) What?

Luke 1 C-can – Come in.

Luke 2 *comes back in.*

Rob *looks at the two of them.*

Rob This one looks knackered.

Luke 1 H-he's from –

Luke 2 I'm from the t-tomorrow you don't want to . . . happen.

Rob Why?

Lukes C-can't tell you.

Beat.

Rob *adjusts his hat.*

Rob   What's with your face?

Beat.

What's wrong with his face?

Luke 1   Can I . . . tell him?

Luke 2   I can't tell you.

Luke 1   B-but –

Luke 2   Do what you . . . feel's best.

Pause.

Luke 1   B-B-B. Ben. Pulled one of my . . . teeth out.

Beat.

Rob   What?

Luke 2 *nods.*

Luke 1   H-he, he –

Rob   Come here.

Luke 2 *wanders over.*

Rob   Let me see.

Luke 2 *opens his mouth.*

Pause.

Luke 1   He . . . wants the . . . b-box.

Luke 2 (*with mouth open*)   Aaaa uhhhh fwaaa.

Luke 1   And the . . . flat.

Greg's with him, t-too.

Luke 2 *closes his mouth.*

Luke 2   We . . . need Greg. He's i-important.

Pause.

Luke 1   You alright?

Rob *suddenly kicks* **The Man** *in the stomach. He whimpers and shrinks away.*

Luke 2   Don't!

Rob   Why didn't you tell me?

Luke 1   Only just . . . happened.

Rob   What? This morning?

Luke 1   Last n-night.

Rob   Why didn't you *tell* me?

Luke 1   He said I couldn't, he said he'd k-kill you. And t-tell the police on you.

Rob   What, after he'd killed me?

Luke 1   No, he / s-said . . . that –

Luke 2   He m-m-means that –

Rob   You *tell* me. When *anything* goes wrong, you tell me, alright?

Luke 1   Y-yeah, but –

Rob   No fucking buts man! No buts! *Tell* me. That means fucking *immediately*.

You can't look after yourself, your head's in the fucking *clouds* all day –

Luke 1   It's your fault!

Beat.

You br-brought him here! It's you th-that makes this . . . f-fucking shit h-happen. All y-you ever do is talk about mistakes – but you keep f-f-fucking *making em*!

If you just stayed . . . a-away from us, then n-none of this would ever h-happen to me. So *y-you* fucking sort it out!

Rob *goes to punch* **Luke 1** *but at the last second switches and punches himself in the face, awkwardly and hard.*

Pause.

His nose is bleeding slightly.

He laughs a little, embarrassed.

Luke 1 *walks away down the corridor.*

Pause.

Luke 2   I didn't m-mean that.

Rob *shoots him a look.*

Blackout.

Three

The same.

About half five, the same day.

Luke 2 *stands looking through a crack in the curtains.*

The Man *is wandering about the room on all fours. He looks at* **Luke 2** *occasionally.*

Luke 2 *stays frozen at the window for a while until –*

Luke 2   Sit still, man. Ann-nnoying.

He turns and leans with his back against the window and rubs his nose.

He checks his watch.

The Man *is hanging around by the table and chairs, looking anxious.*

Pause.

Luke 2   You need to stay out the way later on. That's what you have to . . . do.

Beat.

That's . . . i-important.

Pause.

Do you even . . . understand us? Really?

Pause.

I bet you don't even . . . remember me. Not h-hardly, anyway.

Beat.

Not that it matters.

A silence.

The Man *points at the goldfish on the table.*

He grunts.

Luke 2 *looks up.*

Beat.

What?

Pause.

The Man　Fish bowl.

Pause.

A flicker of something passes over **The Man**'s *face.*

Luke 2 *stands up and approaches* **The Man**.

Luke 2　S-say – Wh-what was that? S-say again.

Nothing.

S-say . . . it again. F-fish bowl.

Nothing.

Wh-what do you m-mean?

Nothing.

C-come on, what was . . . that?

Nothing.

He gives up.

V-v-very useful. Fish bowl.

The buzzer goes.

Luke 2 *jumps.*

He goes to answer it.

Luke 2　H –

Intercom　S'me.

He presses the button and opens the door.

Enter **Rob**.

Rob　You alright?

Luke 2 *looks at* **The Man**.

Rob   What?

Luke 2   S-sorry. Nothing.

Rob   Have you come out your room yet?

Luke 2   N-not yet.

Rob   Fuck's sake. Go and have a word.

Luke 2   I'll . . . try.

Luke 2 *goes off down the corridor.*

Rob *looks around the room, restless.*

He goes to the kitchen and fumbles about in the drawers.

He comes back with a knife.

He mutters something.

He stuffs it down the side of the sofa.

He sits on the sofa and practises pulling it out of the cushion.

Enter **Luke 2**.

Luke 2   He's not sp-speaking to us.

Rob   Best if you stay out of it anyway.

Luke 2   Why've you g-got a –

Rob   Why do you think?

Luke 2   I d-don't –

Rob   Who's got the most experience with dodgy bastards here? (*Beat.*) You or me?

Beat.

Unless you've got a fucking . . . vaporiser or something back there –

Then you're useless to me.

. . .

I used to have an imagination too, you know.

All it does is get you in trouble.

Beat.

Luke 2   I'm not the one that . . . shouted at you.

Rob   Just let us get on with this on my own.

Luke 2   I . . . need to s-say though –

Rob   Just leave it, Luke, man.

Luke 2   But I have to *t-tell* you –

Rob   *Leave* it.

Beat.

Sort this out first, alright?

The Man *has been watching the two of them carefully.*

Beat.

Rob   Want you to go round Greg's and get him over here.

Luke 2   Wh –

Rob   Cos he's been hanging round with this cunt, so we'd best put a stop to that.

He's one of us.

Luke 2   Can't we . . . phone him?

Rob   He's not got a phone.

Luke 2   At h –

Rob   Just go and *get* him. Alright? I'll be fine.

Got moody arse down there if I need you. One of you's more than enough.

Luke 2   I c-can't, you d-don't –

Rob   Fuck's *sake* man! I don't want you here!

Beat.

Luke 2 *looks at his watch.*

Rob   Go!

Luke 2 *heads off, shutting the door behind him.*

Rob (*to* **The Man**)   And you can stop looking at me like that, and all.

Beat.

We don't want him getting involved.

Beat.

It's my mess, I'll clean it up. You just stay out the way.

Pause.

I'm sorry I booted you before.

I'll make it up to you.

He goes to the window.

I'll make everything up to everyone.

He checks his watch.

But we'll fix this first.

Beat.

I'll . . .

He adjusts his hat.

I'm the grown-up round here . . .

Beat.

You jus –

There's a knock at the door.

Rob *looks over.*

Rob   Just keep your head down, alright?

The door opens with another knock.

Enter **Ben.**

Pause.

Ben   Shall we sit and chat?

Rob *nods.*

Ben *shuts the door and goes over to the sofa. He sits where* **Rob** *had planned to sit.*

Rob *stays standing.*

Ben   You don't want to sit?

Rob *shakes head.*

Pause.

Ben   So Luke's filled you in.

Rob   You're not getting it.

Ben   I am, Rob, I'm afraid.

Rob   You're fucking not.

Ben   It doesn't matter how many knives you've hidden in the sofa, I'm still getting what I want.

Beat.

And if you leave, I'll let you be. If you don't, then you'll be hurt.

And Luke will be hurt.

Maybe you'll be killed, I'm not sure. I'll leave it up to them.

Rob   You've bought some new friends, then?

Ben   Yes.

Rob   That the only way you can get respect?

Ben   There's not a shortage of people who'd enjoy hurting you, Rob.

Beat.

The way you go about things;

you've not set your sights on the long term, have you?

You can't just glass everyone you don't get on with.

Rob   You don't –

Ben   And being insane enough to keep a grown man as a pet only gets you so far.

Rob   You still wanted to –

Ben   Just because I wanted to use you, doesn't mean I respected you.

Or even liked you. You were just the bottom rung on the ladder.

You seemed *malleable.*

And there was no reason why we couldn't have kept working together.

Rob   I change my mind about people when they start pulling my brother's teeth out.

Ben   I gave him plenty of opportunity to avoid that.

I offered him a *house* for the pair of you to live in –

But he wasn't interested. He didn't want to live with you.

Rob   Fucking shut up.

Beat.

Ben   I like Luke. He's intelligent, he's quick. He's articulate, despite his problem.

I much prefer him to you.

But he made this very complicated.

Rob   You can't buy everything.

Ben   Of course I can. Especially round here.

And I can certainly buy people to hurt you.

People are willing to do that for free.

I even bought your number one fan.

Rob   He's just simple.

Ben   He has the sense to recognise opportunity.

Rob   He'll come round when he sees what a fucking psycho you are.

Ben   I don't know why you're so quick to label me.

Rob   You pulled my brother's tooth out!

Ben   And you keep your father on a dog lead.

Beat.

So I think you win.

Pause.

Rob, you break things. Everything.

You break relationships. You break *people*.

Only the junkies can stand to be near you.

Your own brother doesn't want you around. And who can blame him?

You're a violent, angry boy. You've broken your father –

Rob   I didn't – He was like that when I found him –

Ben   I doubt he had a lead.

He goes over to **The Man**.

Ben   Are you not done punishing him yet?

Rob You fucking stay away from him.

Ben It makes sense, the control thing. But it's sick.

And Luke says nothing about it.

Rob He barely remembers –

Ben Maybe he's scared of what you could do to him.

Beat.

My dentistry has hurt him far less than any of your decisions.

Beat.

I couldn't even *begin* to replicate the damage you've done.

The buzzer goes.

Beat.

Answer it if you want.

Beat.

Rob *goes over and presses the button.*

Enter **Greg**.

Greg *looks at the two of them.*

Greg What's going on?

Ben How did you know to come here, Greg?

Greg Wh – I got your text.

Ben And who bought you your phone?

Greg / You –

Rob Do you think I fucking care if you bought him a phone?

Ben Christ Rob, do you have to put 'fuck' into *every* sentence?

Who bought you your phone, Greg?

Greg   You did.

Ben   And who's getting you a flat for yourself?

Greg   . . . You are.

Ben   And when you asked Rob here, when you *asked* him if you could do a bit of work for him, what did he say? Bearing in mind, that there's not many who'd offer to work with you, Rob.

Greg   He – He said no.

Ben   Did he just say no? Or was there a 'fuck' in that sentence too?

Greg   Told me to fuck off.

Ben   Of course. Of course he did.

Rob   You want to work for this cunt now?

Greg   He – He pays us.

Rob   That's all you're interested in?

Greg   He – What've you ever done for us?

Rob   I've fucking looked out –

Greg   Naw you haven't! You *haven't*! All you do is call us a dickhead!

Ben *is spinning the dials on the side of the box idly.*

Rob   You – I've *always* –

Greg   You don't do owt! Neither of yous!

I have to do sommit for myself, I have to get myself better off –

Rob   So you're only friends with people who pay you, then?

Ben   Rob, you're repeating yourself.

Rob   Just cos you're some rich cunt from London, doesn't mean you can do what you want – Doesn't mean you can go round pulling people's teeth out.

Ben   I gave Luke a *choice*. He picked the stupid option –

You're not *listening* – I'm trying to come down to your level here, I'm not using any big words – Everyone. Gets. A choice. How about this, do you understand this?

Ben *wraps the lead around* **The Man***'s neck and pulls.*

Rob (*advancing*)   / Don't *touch* him!

Ben (*pulling the lead*)   You *stay* there.

Rob *stops.*

Ben   Now you can walk out of here with your father breathing, or you can both be carried out in bin bags.

Greg   / He can't breathe . . .

Rob   Don't- Don't- Just- Fucking / *leave* him!

Ben   Don't *move*. I *told* you.

He yanks the lead tighter. **The Man** *struggles weakly.*

Rob *squirms on the spot in agony.*

Rob   *Stop* it, man!

Ben   There are *no* second chances.

I offered you *all* more opportunity than you've *ever* had –

Greg   Ben, don't –

Ben (*to* **Greg**)   You *shut* your mouth.

Greg   / But don't do that though –

Rob   *Leave* him!

Ben (*to* **Greg**)   You *remember* who pays you –

Rob   / Fucking let go of him!

Greg   He hasn't done anything though –

Ben (*to* **Greg**)   / I won't tell you again –

Rob   Put him *down*.

Ben   Rob, it's time to choose –

Rob *stumbles over the sofa and tries to grab the stashed knife.*

With a yelp of a laugh, **Ben** *drops the lead and grabs* **Rob** *by the throat, yanking him to his feet.*

The Man *crawls weakly away to a corner.*

Ben   I gave you a *choice*!

Ben *presses* **Rob** *up against the wall, squeezing his throat.*

Ben   And again you pick *violence*. And that's what I *expect* of you.

And that's why you won't ever *win*, Rob.

Because you pick the stupid option every time.

The knife in the sofa. Your dad on a dog lead. Have you ever just *talked* to anyone?

Rob *struggles and punches at* **Ben** *weakly.*

Greg   Let him go man, he's not breathing –

Cords stand out on **Rob**'s *neck as he chokes and grunts.*

Ben   I know you just want the same as everyone else –

A nice house, enough money, and your family around you.

But that will *never* happen. And not because of me, but because of what's inside *you*.

Even if I left, tomorrow there'd be five more *just* like me –

Because this place is *rotting*, and things that rot attract vultures and dogs.

We're the *only* ones interested in you –

Greg   Ben, please –

Ben   And I want you to be aware that this is the option you *chose* for yourself –

He has taken a switchblade out of his pocket. His volume rises.

This is where you've all been heading for *years* –

Luke 1 *hurtles in from the corridor and pulls at* **Ben**.

Luke 1   *LET GO! LET GO OF HIM!*

He screams and kicks at **Ben**, *who wraps his hand around* **Luke 1***'s face and smashes his head into the wall.*

Luke 1 *keeps trying to help his brother but is now dazed and weaker.*

Ben*'s volume rises.*

Ben   *Look* outside. I'm the *best* option available in this *husk* of a town –

Beggars can't be choosers.

And if you aren't strong enough to stop me, you vacant *chav*, then why shouldn't I just *take your nose if I want it*?

Ben *starts cutting* **Rob***'s nose away from his face.*

Greg   *Stop it man!*

Luke 2 *bursts in the front door and hurls himself over the sofa at* **Ben**, *yelling desperately.*

With both **Lukes** *and* **Rob**, **Ben** *has to struggle harder to keep cutting.*

He rants as he fights them off –

Ben   Just *stop*. You *can't win*. You can't stop the inevitable – They chose *ME*.

The struggle goes on, with **Rob** *bellowing as his nose is cut, with* **Luke 1** *trying to pull* **Ben***'s arm away from his brother, with* **Luke 2** *pulling at* **Ben***'s waist and biting his shoulder –*

Greg   *LEAVE EM ALONE!*

Greg *flies into the struggle and pushes* **Ben** *from the front.*

Finally the combined effort is enough, and **Ben**, *mostly propelled by* **Greg**, *falls with a grunt of surprise into the box, where* **Luke 1** *scrambles to punch the large button on the side of it.*

A massive, instant wave of noise tears through the flat, as if the universe has torn in two. Brilliant, blinding white light shoots from the gaps in the box.

Silence.

The box smokes slightly.

The boys stand slowly, speechless.

The only sound is **Rob** *breathing awkwardly through his mutilated nose.*

Pause.

Rob *takes two puffs from his inhaler.*

Rob   Wh . . .

Beat.

Luke 1 *looks at the box.*

Luke 1   He's gone to the year six thousand, two hundred and sixty-eight.

Pause.

Luke 1   Is that –

Luke 2   We didn't get him in last time.

Beat.

We couldn't stop him.

Beat.

Rob *looks over to* **Luke 2**.

Rob   . . . tomorrow . . .

Beat.

Greg *is clutching his arm.*

Greg   I'm bleeding, man. He cut me.

Rob *goes over and looks at* **Greg***'s arm, snorting blood.*

Rob   Let's have a – I can't see it with your hand over it, can I? Sit down.

He sits **Greg** *down on the sofa.*

Greg   He's cut us –

Rob (*to* **Lukes**)   Go and get us some bandages or sommit.

Luke 1   Bandag –

Rob   Some plasters or sommit, go down the shops –

Lukes   Right.

They both rush out the front door, leaving it open.

Rob   Well don't both – Never . . .

Rob *looks at* **Greg***'s arm.*

Greg   There's loads of it . . .

Rob   This is nowt, this.

Greg   Hurts.

Rob   Course it hurts, you knobhead. Just keep your hand on it, it's not deep.

He sits down on the floor by the sofa.

In the scuffle, his hat has been knocked off, and we can see he's balding slightly.

He suddenly looks very old and tired.

Beat.

Dunno what you're complaining about. Half my fucking nose is hanging off.

He touches it.

Greg *is crying.*

Rob   What? What you doing?

Greg   I'm sorry man . . .

Rob   What?

Greg   I'm sorry I was with him and that, I didn't want to be with him, I didn't like him or owt really –

Rob   Come on, pack it in.

Greg   I just wanted to do some work and that cos I wanted money –

I didn't want him to hurt yous –

I just don't have anything else –

Rob   Alright, man.

Greg *(sniffs)*   I just wanted something to happen –

Rob   I know man, calm down.

Greg   I'm sick of being nothing . . .

Rob   It's alright.

Beat.

He pats **Greg***'s leg.*

Rob   Let's all just calm down for a minute.

Pause.

You were a bit like Darth Vader weren't you?

Greg *(sniffs)*   Eh?

Rob   Cos you were bad, but then you chucked him in there at the end.

Greg   Oh right, yeah. I was a bit. (*Sniffs.*) Were you Han Solo?

Beat.

Rob   Naw.

I was just a fucking idiot.

Like I always have been.

Pause.

Greg   What do you reckon it looks like? In the future?

Rob   Round here?

. . .

I'd be surprised if there was even dust left.

Pause.

Greg   Is your dad alright, Rob?

Rob *looks over at* **The Man**, *who is curled up in a corner.*

Rob   He'll just be asleep –

Beat.

He gets up awkwardly and walks over to **The Man**.

Pause.

He kicks him lightly with his shoe.

Rob   Come on, you lazy get.

Pause.

He crouches next to **The Man**.

He puts a hand on **The Man**'s *face.*

Pause.

Rob *wraps his head in his arms.*

He rocks.

Pause.

Greg (*quietly*)   I'll go get Luke, Rob. I'll go get him.

He hurries out of the flat.

Pause.

Rob *picks up* **The Man**.

Rob *holds his father.*

A silence.

He puts him down.

He stands up.

Pause.

He looks at the fish.

He goes to the kitchen.

He comes back with a jug.

He scoops the fish and some of the water into the jug and stands it on the table.

He picks up the bowl and carries it through to the kitchen.

We watch through the serving hatch as he tips the water into the sink.

Pause.

He comes back into the room.

He puts the bowl on his head.

Pause.

He takes his phone out of his pocket, looks around, and then stuffs it under the sofa cushion.

He looks at his watch.

He goes over to the box and turns the dials.

He gently picks his father up.

He stands, looking around the room.

He looks at the door, as if waiting for someone.

Pause.

He carries his father into the box.

He reaches his hand out from within and presses the button.

A massive, instant wave of noise tears through the flat, as if the universe has torn in two. Brilliant, blinding white light shoots from the gaps in the box.

Pause.

Both **Lukes** *and* **Greg** *come rushing back in.*

Luke 1   Wh –Wh –

Greg   He was here man, and your dad's – Maybe he's –

He runs down the corridor, calling **Rob**'s *name.*

Luke 2   W-where are they . . .

Greg *comes back.*

Greg   He's not – Maybe he went to –

Luke 1 *is touching the box.*

Beat.

Greg   Has he . . .

Luke 1 *looks at the dials.*

Luke 1   Nineteen ninety.

Beat.

Greg   Do you think he's gone . . .

Pause.

Luke 2   N-no –

He can't . . . have –

He looks at his watch.

We got him in there this time –

We s-saved em –

W-w-we *fixed* it –

We *stopped* him –

I came *back*, and –

. . .

He's –

Maybe he's –

Luke 2 *rushes out the front door. We hear him calling* **Rob**'s *name.*

Luke 1 *has his hands on his head.*

Luke 2 *is shouting and yelling outside.*

Pause.

Luke 1 *goes over to the box and folds it away. He hurls it down the corridor.*

Luke 2's *yelling stops.*

A silence.

Greg   Luke, man . . .

I –

Rob*'s phone under the sofa cushion starts to ring.*

Pause.

Luke *looks under the sofa, then pulls the sofa cushions off and finds the phone.*

He looks at it.

He stands up.

Greg   Who is it?

Beat.

Luke *answers it.*

Luke   H-hello?

He listens as someone speaks at length. He nods occasionally.

Okay.

Pause.

Okay.

Pause.

Alright.

He rubs tears from his eyes impatiently.

I know.

Pause.

Okay.

He hangs up.

Pause.

Greg   Who was it?

Beat.

Luke   V-v-v-that . . . I-i-i-t was . . .

Beat.

That was . . . H-h-he said . . .

He shakes his head with frustration.

Beat.

That was . . .

He takes a breath to speak –

Blackout.

Notes

Luke has a speech impediment that consists mainly of not being able to get each word out of his mouth without a gap. These gaps are indicated with a ' . . . ', which means in his speech, ' . . . ' can indicate either a trailing off or a struggle to speak. A trailing off will most frequently occur at the end of a train of thought, and it should be easy enough to distinguish what's what.

It's indicated clearly where he stutters, stammers or pauses, but the actor should be free to use his discretion as to where a tic may or may not occur, keeping in mind the pace of the play, and that the audience will want to go home at some point.

THE TWO LUKES

It's not essential that the Lukes be identical, but rather that they have a similar 'spark'. The confusion in the audience when a different actor comes on as Luke in Act Two should work in favour of the tone.

ACCENT

The Middlesbrough accent is often lumped together with Geordie, when it's very different. Several words have been contracted within the script (e.g. 'Something' to 'Sommit'), but overall I leave the accenting up to the cast, and it should be pretty clear if they have a grasp of how the natives speak.

PARMO

A chicken parmesan, or 'parmo', is a local delicacy consisting of a flat, fried chicken breast in breadcrumbs, coated in béchamel sauce, then cheese, then grilled to perfection. Served in a pizza box with chips and salad.

Captain Amazing

with illustrations by Rebecca Glover

for mark
for clive
for gez

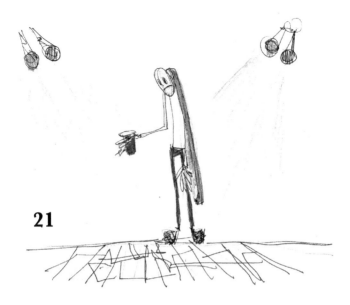

21

– It's a cape.

– It's a *cape*.

– What?

– It's a *cape*, what I'm wearing is a cape.

– It's – This is a shit song. I hate this song, don't you hate
 this song?
– I don't mind.
– It's a shit song. You asked what I was wearing –
– It's a cape, fine.
– You want to know why I'm wearing it?
– What?
– I said, you want to know why I'm wearing a cape?

– I'm a superhero.

– I'm a *superhero*. Can you hear me?
 Can you *hear* me?

1

–   Sorry – Excuse me?
–   Mm?
–   Do you know where I can get a, uh, I need some *sealant* –
–   Sealant.
–   Yes –
–   What kind of –
–   I have a crack in my – My *sink* has a crack in it, and –
–   Your sink?
–   Yes.
–   Bathroom sink?
–   Yes.
–   Sealant won't really . . . It's a normal – ?
–   A porcelain type of a –
–   Right, bathroom sink.
–   I heard I can get some stuff to kind of, ah, *goop* into it.

–   Goop?

–   Sorry, that's stupid.

–   Uh – Well you can't really get a – How big is this crack?
–   Like – This?
–   Yeah, you can't really – We have this, but it's really just
        for painting onto tiny chips. You can't really goop it
        into big cracks.
–   We don't have to keep saying goop . . .

–   Are you renting . . . ?
–   No, I – I've just bought my first house –
–   So you won't lose your deposit then.
–   No. I just might need another sink.
–   Yeah, you probably will.

–   What?
–   Sorry.
–   You're still laughing.
–   Sorry.
–   It wasn't that funny.
–   I know, sorry.

–   Sorry.

–   What's your name?
–   I've got my –
–   Oh, yeah. Right on your – That's stupid.
–   It's alright.

–   . . .
–   . . .

–   Do you live nearby?
–   Just – Yes. Five minutes away?

–   . . .
–   . . .
–   Do you need anything else?
–   No. No, thank you.
–   Okay.
–   Alright.

–   Well. Bye.
–   Bye.

- You'll never get away with this Evil Man!
- Oh won't I? You're awfully confident for someone tied to the biggest bomb in the world, Dr Scientist Man. We'll see how sure you are once I've blown up the whole world –

  Which won't be very sure, because you'll be dead.
- It's only a matter of time before Captain Amazing comes here to stop you –
- I don't think we need to worry about our friend Captain Amazing, Dr Scientist – You see, I chained him to a rocket and launched it directly into the sun. I hope he packed his sun cream – Say – Factor Two Billion?

  Ahahahahahaha!
- Sorry I'm late!
- Captain Amazing!
- Gah! Curses! Not this bell end!
- Your scheme might have worked had I not been invincible against the sun, Evil Man. As it is, I just got a light tan.

—   You look great!
—   You're too late Amazing, I've already started the countdown. When this bomb goes off the whole planet will lose their heads – Literally.
—   I'm getting pretty tired of this shit, Evil Man.
—   And just to be safe, I've sealed the override switch in this diamond-plated granite safe!
—   Well there's one thing you hadn't counted on –
—   That'd be two things by this point –
—   There's two things you hadn't counted on – My laser eyes can burn through diamond and granite no problem.
—   You're foiled now, Evil Man!
—   Well I'll just have to launch the bomb manually! Ahahahahahaha!
—   After him Captain!
—   I'm going, I'm going –
—   You'll never defeat me –
—   You haven't a chance, Evil Man –

—   Ahahahaha! Once again you're too late Amazing!
—   Stop being a *dick*!
—   Argh!
—   Take this!
—   Gah –
—   And this!
—   Argg –
—   And that one was buy one get one *free* –
—   Nooooooo . . .
—   Captain Amazing! The bomb! It's launching!
—   Do you not think I can see that?
—   But I'm still tied to it!
—   Christ –
—   Captain Amaaazzziiinnnnggggg . . .
—   Hold on!

3

– This is nice.
– Yeah, it's alright.
– There's not many places left round here that aren't
        chains –
– Oh, it's a chain.
– Oh, right.
– Do you not like –
– No it's – I'm not being a snob or –
– Okay.
– I've just never been in –
– I've got vouchers, so –

– What?
– Nothing.

– What's funny?
– Nothing. I'm hungry.

– Can we uh – Can we get whatever we want, or do the
        vouchers – ?
– Just get what you – The vouchers aren't a big –
    I probably shouldn't have even said . . .

–   It's fine.

–   The lobster looks nice.

–   Uh – where's the – ?
–   I'm joking about the lobster.
–   If you want lobster . . .
–   No, I don't, I was just –

–   I don't want lobster.
–   Well if you do.
–   It's not even on the menu, I was just . . .

–   This is going badly isn't it?
–   No, no, it's not –
–   I'm sorry if this is shit.
–   It's not shit.
–   I don't go out with people very often, so –
–   This is fine –
–   You can leave if you want.
–   I won't,
     judge you.
     If that's what you want.
–   It's not.
     You're sweet.
–   Sweet?
–   Not in a – an *emasculating* –
–   Emasculating.
–   Nono, I mean –
–   What's emasculating mean?
–   Nothing. Nothing.
–   Are you alright?
–   Yes, fine. I've just got the giggles.

- And it's had one previous owner.
- What's the reason for selling?
- Retirement. It's in very good condition for the price.

- Are these the original beams?
- I can check that for you.
- Obviously a benefit is the open top, so you can just fly
  straight in, no need for a front door.
  Although, if an emergency does occur, there's a thirty-
  inch thick steel shield that slides across at the flick of
  a switch.

- And the volcano is inactive.
- Completely. It's not actually a volcano, it's just been
  designed to look as such to deter trespassers. And for
  the ambience.
  And, as we mentioned, there are fifteen bedrooms,
  twelve bathrooms, a control room, a missile silo with

four active nuclear warheads, and forty-eight holding
pens.
- Holding pens?
- Basically a dungeon.
- It has a dungeon?
- I can show you if you'd –
- I don't – I'm not sure this is what I'm looking for . . .
- It's a very good price for what you're getting.
- Who was the previous owner?
- See, I'm afraid I can't *name* the seller for various reasons –
- What was his occupation?
- He was a villain.
- A villain?
- An evil genius.
- Right –
- But I assure you, once you've had a look around you'll
see it can be easily refitted for your needs.
- I just – I'm really more in the market for a purpose-built
superhero headquarters.
- Yes.
- I'm not really looking for a doer-upper.
- Right, yes.
- I just don't think I'll have any use for a missile silo or
a dungeon.
- Mm-hm.
- I'm looking more for a Fortress of Solitude type of
a property.
- I could check if Superman's interested in selling?
- No, just something *like* that. I don't – Somewhere a bit
closer to home than the Arctic.
- Okay, well, why don't we shoot back to the office and
look over some more suitable properties?

- Sir?
- I don't know. I'm starting to think this might be an
unnecessary expense.

5

—   This is it then.
—   Yeah, I suppose it's – Do you want a tea?
—   Okay.

—   It's pretty sparse.
—   What?
—   You don't really have much – furniture, or –
—   I don't really have many guests.

—   Do you have another chair?
—   What?
—   Do you just have one chair, or?
—   I think I might have – There's one upstairs, or –
—   No, it's alright.
—   I can just –
—   It's fine.

—   I'll stand.

—   Bit embarrassed.
—   Don't – It's fine. It's – uncluttered.

– This what you're reading?
– Yeah, it's just a – a western.
– You like westerns?
– They're alright.
– You read a lot?
– I try to –
– Do you have a lot of books, or?
– I just use the library.
– So it's just this one book.
– I read one and take it back and get another.
– Are you a monk, or?
– A monk?
– I've never seen such a – You don't have anything.
– I just don't feel the need to have much.
 We can go out if you want.
– No, it's fine.

– I'm going to buy you a lamp or something.
– It's light enough.
– It's like a cell.
 Did you buy those curtains?
– They were just here when I moved in.
– You're not a big decorator.
– Not – Not really.
– But you work – I mean, you sell people –
– Stuff to do up their houses, yeah.
– But you've never been tempted.
– No. I don't really – It's fine. Sorry.
– It's just really lonely. Makes me sad.

– Oh, I got you these.
 You know.
– What for?
– Well, it's just.
 Been a few months now, hasn't it.

–   You've been counting?
–   Not – Counting, but. I've got a fair idea. Few months.

–   They alright?
–   They're lovely.

–   I like it. This. Us.

–   Me too.

6

–   This ends *here*, Evil Man! I've foiled your plots to blow
    up the world, to turn everyone in the world into your
    slaves, and your plot to give everyone an arse for a
    face. Now I've cornered you in this burning building
    it's *over*. I'm sick of it.
–   Fine. Do your worst Amazing.
–   Oh right, you're sorry now, are you?
–   You just don't understand. You have no idea.
–   Oh, I've got plenty of ideas. Ideas of how to punch you
    in the face.
–   I wasn't always evil you know. I used to have a different
    life, before all of this, before all of these plots.
–   Pull the other one.
–   Before I was known as Evil Man, my name was Good
    Man. And I was the most good person in the world.
–   I don't believe it.
–   It's true. Check my driver's licence. I was Good Man.

And I was married to a beautiful princess, and we had
three small puppies who were always licking my face.
– What happened?
– One night I was rescuing some orphans from a factory,
and I accidentally fell into a barrel of Evil Juice. I
didn't know it, but the Evil Juice was made of acid
and fire and Hitler's poop. When I swam out of the
Evil Juice I realised that my whole face had changed
and become evil. And so had my brain. I went home
to my Princess wife, but she just slammed the door in
my face because I ate our three puppies, because I
was evil.
– Well. That is a sad story. But it still doesn't excuse what
you've done to this planet. Sometimes bad things
happen. But you can't take those bad things out on
other people.
– I know that, don't you think I know that? I've made
mistakes Amazing –
– We should probably head outside, the fire's spread to
the roof now.
– Of course I've made mistakes. But it's so hard to be
good, when the whole world expects you to be Evil.
– Can't you give me another chance Amazing? As we
stand here, man to man, in this burning house?
Amazing?
Amazing?
Are you listening?

7

– Pregnant.
– Yes.
– Pregnant with a –
– With a baby.
– With a –
– With a *person*, yes.

– You already –
– I went and I had the *scan*, and –
– So you've known –
– I didn't tell you because I didn't want to have the
    conversation where you say 'Let's think about this'
    which actually means 'Let's think about abortion'.
– I wouldn't –
– Because we're not. I'm keeping – She's staying.
    And you can be involved,

Or not.
You can stay or go but you can't –
It's happening.
This is a, a, *thing* –
That's happening.

– She's a she already.
– It's a girl.
– They can tell this soon?
– No, they didn't – I just know.
– You know it's a girl?
– Yes.
– You're guessing.
– I just know.

– You're not saying anything . . .
– Because I'm – I'm just a little bit, uh, *surprised* –
– Shell-shocked.
– I would have said surprised –
– Because you're –
– Because I'm not very articulate, I know –
– I wasn't – saying that –
– It's alright.
– Okay.

– Sorry.

– I'm sorry I didn't tell you. Before.

– Do you hate me?

– What?
– Do you hate me now?
– Of course not.

–   No?
–   No. Course not. I'm just, you know –

–   I mean. Do you *want* me to stay?
–   Do I *want* you to stay.
–   You said I could stay or go, do you *want* me to stay?
–   Of course I do.

–   Okay.

–   Okay?
–   Just. Of course. Yes.
    Three of us.

–   I was really hoping you'd say that.

Ball.

Ball . . .

Ball.

Uh –
Carpet.

Car-pitt.

Ball.

Chair.

You sit in chairs.

See?

Chair.

Tree.

Tree.

Trees grow out of the ground –
And, uh –
Through something called photo-syn-the-sis –
They turn sun – That's the sun –
Into food. Tree food.
Or – Wait –
Or they turn carbon diox-ide –
Into oxygen.
Which we breathe.
And that makes us alive.
It's one of those two, I don't, uh . . .

Ball.

Trousers.

Men wear trousers – And –
Well.
People wear trousers.
Sometimes girls wear trousers too –
You can wear trousers when you grow up, if you want –
Now. You can wear them now. Wear what you want.

Shoes.

Daddy is wearing shoes.

Daddy.

Da-dee.

Daddy wears shoes.

–   Dog.
–   Dog, yes.

–   Dog.
–   Dog.

–   Dog.
–   Yes. Okay.
–   Dog.
–   We don't have a dog, sweetheart.

–   No.

–   Okay.

–   No.
–   No?
–   No.
–   Okay.

–   No.
–   No wh –
–   Dog.
–   Dog again.
–   No.
–   Daddy?

–   Dad?

–   Daddy?
–   Dog.
–   Daddy.
–   Dog.

–   Daddy?
–   No.
–   Okay.

10

- What if no one likes me?
- Well – They'll like you. People will like you.
- What if they don't?
- There's a lot of kids here. I'm sure someone will like you.
  . . .
  They'll like you, of course they'll like you.
- What if the teachers don't like me.
- The teachers have to like you, it's their job. They have
    to like everybody.
- What if the teacher thinks I'm not doing any work and
    I get told off.
- Well do your work, then.
- What if the teacher thinks I'm not doing it but I am.
- Well they won't think that then.
- What if they do and I get told off and expelled.
- I don't –
- What if that happens?
- I don't think that'll happen.

–   It might.
–   I doubt it. Just don't – You'll have fun. It's good.
       School's good.

–   Can you come in with me?
–   No.
–   Why?
–   Because. School's for children. I've done school.
       I finished.
–   Did you ever get told off at school?
–   N – Well – Sometimes.
–   Why?
–   Because I wasn't working hard enough –
–   Why not?
–   Because I was stupid.
–   Why?
–   I don't know why. I just was.
–   But not now.
–   Sometimes now too.
–   You're stupid now?
–   Sometimes. Everyone is sometimes.

–   Are you crying?
–   No.
–   Why are you crying?
–   I'm not.
–   You are.
–   My eyes are just watering.
–   They're not.
–   It's windy, and – It's the wind.
–   What are you crying about?
–   Nothing. I'm not.

–   I'm not.

–   Now you better – You don't wanna be late.

—   Will you pick me up?
—   Mum'll pick you up.
—   What time?
—   Just after three.
—   Three fifteen.
—   Yes.
—   What if she's late?
—   She won't be.
—   What if she's late and I get kidnapped.
—   I don't – That's not – Don't talk to strangers.
—   I don't.
—   Then you won't –
—   What if they just pick me up and run away with me?
—   Just – That won't happen.
—   It might.
—   Well – Just don't talk to strangers.

—   Come on, the bell went already.

—   Bye Dad.

—   Bye.

  . . .

  . . .

  . . .

11

- And that's the last time I tumble dry my costume.
- Mm-hm.
- Do you realise how hard it is to fight crime, when your
    costume's so tight your balls are practically inside
    your anus?

  I don't need to give the Joker any *more* reasons to laugh,
    you know what I'm saying?
- Hm.
- So what's going on with you?
- Not much –
- Did I tell you the fucking batmobile broke down *again*?
- No –
- Right in the middle of a high-speed chase, it just – frrt –
    stops.
- Do you want another beer?
- No I'm fine – I had to continue the chase in the bat jet.
- Okay.
- But my insurance is starting to go through the roof, I've
    had it towed three times this month alone. Maybe I
    should just start using the bat bike more often. But
    obviously it's not as heavily armoured as the car so it's
    like hello, anyone order a sitting duck? You know?

What's wrong with you?
- I'm just bored.
- Of what?
- Of listening to you.
- . . . What?
- Do you realise why Superman never wants to hang out with you any more?
- He sometimes –
- It's because he's sick – we're *all* sick of listening to you moan about how hard it is to be Batman.
- We're talking here –
- No, *you're* talking, I'm struggling to care –
- Hey, come on –
- You were lucky anyone was willing to spend time with you in the first place, and now you've totally outstayed your welcome.
- What's that supposed to mean?
- It means you forced your way into our circle.
- Your circle?
- No one wanted you around, you're not a superhero.
- Oh, I'm not a superhero.
- No.
- Okay.
- You're not.
- Sure, I'm not a superhero.
- No.
- You think I like to wear all this leather for fun?
- Maybe. I don't know.
- I'm out there *every* night, keeping the peace.
- Alright –
- Dealing with the scum of the streets –
- With what?
- What?
- What are you using to combat all this crime?
- I'm –
- What powers do you have?
- Oh come on –
- What powers do you have?

- I'm sick of justifying myself to you fascists.
- I'm saying. Superheroes like hanging out with
      superheroes. We share common ground.
- I share common ground.
- You're just a billionaire with a leather fetish.
- Hey take that back!
- We only put up with you because you buy all the drinks.
- Fuck you Amazing! I know you're just jealous.
- Course I am.
- I'm sorry if I want to talk about real crime fighting,
      instead of listening to you whine about your marriage.
- Okay –
- 'My wife hates me.' 'We never talk any more.'
- Shut up –
- 'Everything's different now.'
- What would you know, bachelor?
- Whatever – I don't need to sit here and listen to this
      I've got work to do –
- Counting your millions of dollars?
- No, I have to go and pick up the dry cleaning for the
      Justice League, which I am a part of, because I'm a
      fucking *superhero*!

12

— So your mum and I –
— Put that down sweetheart –
— We –
— Emily –
— What?
— You have to listen, this is important.
— I can't get –
— Just put it down.

— So me and your mum –
— Your dad and I are going to separate.

— What's that?
— . . .
— That means we're not going to live together any more.

— What?
— No – Sweetheart –
— You're moving away?

–   No – Not away –
–   Your dad's going to rent the house next door, and –
–   Why?
–   Because – It's a very complicated –
–   You hate each other.
–   No! Nonononono –
–   We don't *hate* each other.
–   We just . . . *Think* that – We don't get along as well as
        we used to, and –
–   It's making us sad, and we don't want to make *you* sad –
–   You're making me sad right now.
–   It'd make you more sad if we didn't do this.
–   Why?
–   Because . . .
–   Because we'd be arguing all the time, and –
–   Why?
–   Because we feel angry with each other a lot –
–   Why?
–   Because –
–   What did you do?
–   No one *did* anything –
      It's just –
      Grown-ups sometimes have to do this.
–   Why?
–   Just . . . Because.

–   You'll still see your dad every day.
–   No I won't.
–   Course you will. Won't she?
–   Yeah. Course. Of course.
–   He's just living next door.
–   No he's not.
–   Well he will be.

–   Are you getting divorced?
–   You know what divorced means?

—   We're not – It's sort of – Yes.
—   We are?
—   (I'm just trying to explain it . . .)
—   And you don't love each other.
—   No, we – We still do.
—   Course.
—   You don't.
—   Emily –
—   I don't think you do.
—   Well. We do.
—   Then why can't you live in this house?
—   Because . . . Life is strange sometimes.

—   Why?
—   Stop asking why all the time please sweetheart.
—   But I don't understand.
—   Well. You will. Won't she?
       Hm?
—   Yeah.
       . . .
       Yes.

13

– This is your room.

– It's big. It's quite a big room, so –
– Is this my duvet?
– Yeah, that's – It's Spider-Man.
– Yeah.
– You like Spider-Man.
– He's okay.
– He's okay. Well.
– I have a duvet.
– Yes.
– In Mum's house.
– Well now you've got two.

– Okay.
– Okay?
– Okay.

– How come I don't have a grandma or grandad?
– What?
– How come?
– I –
– They're dead.

- Well – Most of them.
- Not all?
- My dad is still –
- He's not dead?
- No, but –
- Can we meet him?
- I don't think so.
- Why?
- Because we had an argument.
- About what?
- Lots of things. He drinks too much.
- Too much alcohol.
- Yes.
- And that's why.
- Lots of reasons.
- Isn't it better to make up with people.
- Yes. Course.
- So why don't you.
- Because it's complicated.
- Why?
- Because – Come on. Emily.

- I thought we could have a special tea.

- Emily?
- Like what?
- Like a Chinese takeaway.
- I don't know what that is.
- It's food from China.
- How does it get here?
- Well they make it here, and then –
- Then how is it Chinese?
- Because Chinese people – Uh – It – It just is.

- It's cold in this house.

–   Well . . . why don't we wrap you up in your duvet?

–   That better?
–   (*Nods.*)
–   In your duvet suit.
–   Like a cape.
–   Like a cape.

14

- Do you remember how you felt before it happened?
- (*Shakes head.*)
- No?
- Did you feel sick?
- (*Shrugs.*)
- Did you get dizzy?
- (*Shrugs.*)
- You don't remember anything?
- (*Shakes head.*)
- All we want to do is work out what happened so that it
    doesn't happen again.
- Did you see any flashing lights?
- (*Shrugs.*)
- Flashing lights?
- Epilepsy.
- She didn't have a fit –
- Well I'm just trying –
- Don't get worked up –

—   I'm not, but you –
—   Stop fighting.

—   Sorry.
—   Sorry.
—   I won't do it again.
—   Do what?
—   I won't fall over again.

15

- You're younger than most dads.
- Yes.
- Why?
- Just because.
- You had me younger.
- Yes.
- By having sex.
- Well. Yes. We don't need to –
- So that's why you're younger.
- Yes.
- But you're still bald.
- Well, not –
- No superheroes are bald.
- No?
- No.
- I bet some are –
- No. Lex Luthor is. But he's a bad –
- He's a baddie, yes.
- Dr Charles Xavier is bald.
- Who's he?

- He's the dad of the X-Men.
- Well there you are.
- But he doesn't do much. He's in a wheelchair because he's a cripple.
- Don't say cripple sweetheart.
- Well he is.
- You don't say 'cripple'.
  Some words hurt people's feelings.
  Like cripple.
  And bald.
- Was I an accident?
- What?
- Daniel at school said I was an accident.
- Well he should mind his own fucking business.
- Don't swear Dad.
- Sorry.
- So I am?
- No, that's not –
- So you did want me?
- We want you *now* –
- But not before.
- No, that's not –
- You didn't want me before?
- If you let me speak for five seconds I'll tell you.
  Alright?
  You talk too much.
- Mum says I'm curious.
- Well I say you talk too much.
- Mum says I have to talk to you to make us have a better relationship.

- Dad?
- I'm thinking. Hang on.

- Look, sometimes –
  Sometimes things you –
  Not everything that's *meant* to happen is good.
  And sometimes –

Sometimes things that happen by accident –
Those things can be wonderful.

Alright?

Okay.

16

–   Okay –
      Thanks for –
–   Not at all –
–   I just thought it'd be good to, to *touch base*.
–   Yes.

–   So, I mean –
      We *absolutely* appreciate you coming back –
      Of course we do.
      Of course.
      It's just –
      Well.
      We worry –
      We're somewhat, ah, *concerned* – That you might not be
         ready to come back to work for us.

–   Okay.
–   I know, of course, that you've had a tough time recently –
      You know we all know that.
      And maybe, sometimes, just, you know, getting back on
         the old horse is the way forward.
      But we feel there's certain –

Ah –
We're concerned that you're maybe not quite prepared
    ah, *emotionally*.
Yes.

–   So . . . ?
–   So, I, *we*, think,
    maybe
    you should go home.

–   Now?
–   Well not this *second* –
    But,
    today.

–   So I'm fired?
–   No! Nonononono –
    No one's firing anyone here Mark.
–   Captain Amazing.

–   I'm sorry?
–   Captain Amazing.

–   Yes. Well. No one's firing anyone here . . .
–   . . .
–   . . .
–   Captain –
–   Captain Amazing. Yes. We just feel that maybe,
    you take –
    some *time*,
    Until you feel that you can come to work, perhaps . . .
        not wearing the cape.

–   You don't like my cape?

–   Oh!
      It's not that we don't like it Mar – Captain.
      It's just,
      Well.
      We do have uniform regulations here.
–   I'm still wearing the uniform.
–   Yes.
–   Just got the cape on –
–   Over the top, yes.
–   Because I need to wear my cape.
–   But at work . . . ?
–   At work, not at work, everywhere.
–   I see.
–   I'm a superhero.
–   . . .
–   The cape sort of goes with that.
–   You . . . need it to fly?
–   I don't need it to fly, it's just a cape – Capes don't make
          people fly –
–   Oh, no –
–   I don't need it to fly Mike, I can fly without the cape.
      It's just a, a, a, *visual* thing. It lets people know.

–   That you're a superhero –
–   That I'm a superhero, yes.
      I don't need a cape to *fly*, Mike.
–   No, sorry.
–   You fucking idiot.
–   I'm sorry Captain.
–   You don't have a clue do you?
–   Now come on, this is hard for everyone.
–   Doesn't seem too hard for you.
–   Now –
–   It *should* be. It *should* be hard.
–   It is.

–   Do you know how many managers would like to have a
       superhero on their payroll?
    A lot. A lot. And I think it's,
    Extremely short-sighted of you to let one slip through
       your fingers.
    The potential benefits here that you're not – You know.

–   Captain –

–   And who the fuck are you to ask me about my emotional
       state?

–   I, I –

–   I could burn this place to the ground with my heat
       vision, do you really think it's a good idea to piss me
       off?

–   Okay, let's –

–   You should be doing *everything* in your power to keep me
       happy,
    But you're too *stupid* to even realise what you've got in
       front of you.
    You're an *ant*.
    You're *nothing*.
    I'm a *god*. I'm fucking *Hercules*.
    You'd have to be *insane* to let me just walk out your
       door.

    Don't you think?

17

–   Alright. You're going to sleep.
–   I bet I won't.
–   You will.
–   I won't.
–   You want the door open?
–   Will you read me a story?
–   No, it's late.
–   Please?
–   You said you'd go straight to sleep if I let you stay up.
–   Yeah –
–   And I did. So. That's your side of the bargain.
–   But –
–   That's your side. It's late. What time is it?
–   It's not that late.
–   It's late.

–   I'm not reading anything long.
–   No.
–   Get your shortest –

–   Make up a story.
–   That's not reading, is it?
–   It's easier.
–   No it's not.
–   But –
–   Emily –
–   Please.

–   About what? Who's it about, you?
–   No.
–   Who's it about?
–   I don't know. You.
–   Me? You don't want to hear a story about me.
–   I do.
–   I don't have any stories that are –
–   You have to make one up.

–   About what?
–   Use your imagination!

–   Are you a superhero?
–   What?
–   Do you have powers? That can be the story.
–   Fine. Yes.
–   You've got powers.
–   Yes.
–   Like what?
–   Just, you know. All of them.
–   You have to be specific.
–   That's a good word. How long have you been saying
        specific?
–   It's just a word.
–   I'm impressed.
–   You're impressed by anything. What are your powers?
–   I don't know . . . I can fly. I guess.

–   You can fly.
–   And fire . . . things from my eyes . . .
–   Lasers.
–   Fine. Lasers.
–   And what else?
–   . . . See through walls . . . and . . .
–   Dad you're falling asleep.
–   I'm not . . .
–   Dad.
–   I'm resting my eyes. I'm listening.
–   What's your name?
–   What?
–   Your name as a superhero.
–   Just, you know . . . Captain . . .

–   Captain What?
–   Amazing. Mr Amaz – Captain Amazing.

–   That's the worst name Dad.
–   It's fine . . .
–   That's the worst superhero name ever made.
        What do you do as Captain Amazing?
–   Fight . . . baddies and things. Save people.
        . . . make people go to bed when they're supposed to
        go to bed . . .
        . . .
        . . .
–   Dad?

–   Are you asleep?

–   Dad?

–   Good night.

–   . . .
–   . . .

–   Hey-

–   Hey. Superman –
–   . . .
–   Superman –
–   Oh! Captain Amazing, Hi!
–   I was trying to – But –
–   Yeah, yeah. The wind, you know.
–   I can't hear a fucking thing.
–   How've you been?
–   Wha?
–   *How've you been?*
–   Oh, fine, fine.
–   I heard you and Mrs Amazing-?
–   Yeah, we've separated.

–   Sorry to hear that.
–   What?
–   *I said I'm sorry to hear that.*
–   It's okay. It was probably time.

–   How's your kid?
–   Oh, yeah, she uh –
–   She's at school now?
–   Yeah, just started.
–   How's she – Ah!

–   You alright?
–   Fucking birds.
–   Tell me about it.

–   Well. I'd better go.
–   Alright.
–   I'd stay and chat, but –
–   I know you're busy. Nice to see you.
–   You too man. I'll see you around.

19

–   Emily –
–   Emily can you put that –
–   Emily, listen.

–   We –
–   Every time we sit like this you tell me something bad.
–   Well, that's –
–   Every time!

–   Look –
–   What?
–   Emily.

–   The Doctor says –
–   Can I go back to school?
–   Well, that's what we're – Can you help me out here?
–   Sweetheart –

– The Doctor says it's going to take a bit longer.
 And that's why –
 You know.

– So he says we have to work hard to make you, to get
  better.
– Work hard?
– Yes.
– You have to be strong.
– I'm not strong.
– Course you are.
– I can't even open the jam.
– Not that kind of – Like a different strong.
– Headstrong.
– Headstrong.
– Strong in the head?
– Yes.
– Like headbutting things.
– No –
– Just brave. It just means brave.
– Why do I have to be brave?
– Because you're poorly.
– I get poorly all the time.

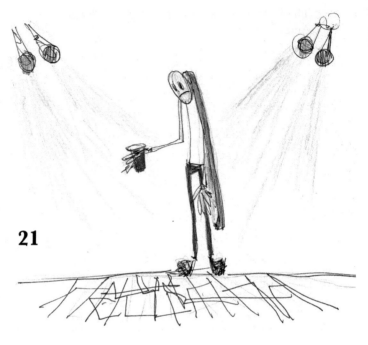

21

–   I'm a superhero.

–   I'm a *superhero*. Can you hear me?
–   Can you hear me?
–   Hey –
–   Can you please leave me alone?
–   We're just having a conversation –
–   No, you're just shouting at me.
–   Sorry.
–   Drunk.
–   I'm just telling you –
–   I don't care what you're dressed as.
–   I'm not *dressed* as anything, I'm Captain Amazing.
–   Okay. Fine. Go away.
–   I'm the real thing –
–   Leave her alone, mate.

- I'm just having a conver*sation*, why's everyone –
- Go *away* –
- You don't have to be such a bitch about it –
- Piss off –
- Alright mate, time to leave.
- We're *talking* here –
- Outside.

–   I'm always asleep.
–   That's okay.
–   It's boring.
–   It's not boring if you're asleep, is it?
–   Yes.
–   How can it be if you're sleeping?

–   It's boring being tired all the time.

–   Are you tired now?
–   (*Nods.*)

–   Am I more like you or more like Mum?
–   You're, ah, more like your Mum. You're better than me.
–   I'm not like you?
–   Well, okay, you've got – You've got bits of both of us.
       But you got most of your good bits from Mum.
–   Mum says you don't like yourself very much.
–   Well Mum – tells you things I wish she wouldn't.
–   Why don't you?
–   I do – I mean – I'm alright. Don't worry about me.
–   Sometimes I do.

–   Worry?
–   (*Nods.*)
–   About what?
–   That you're sad. You're sad all the time.

–   Well don't.
     Just –
     Concentrate on yourself.

–   Dad?
–   What?
–   I'm sorry I'm so boring.
–   You're not boring, stop saying that.
–   All I do is sleep and be sick.
–   That's fine.
     That's enough.

–   Do you know what's going to happen next?

–   No.

–   I don't.
–   But no one knows sweetheart.
     Not even your doctor.
     No one knows anything either way.

     I know I'm your dad and that means I should know
        everything,
     But,
     I just don't.
     I don't know.
     . . .
     I used to think my dad knew everything.
     I used to think he was indestructible.

Built from bricks and stone.
And it's hard – when you find out that's not true,
But it happens to everyone.
It's just happened to you a bit sooner than most.
. . .
But none of that means I won't be here with you.
Whatever happens,
Me and your mum will be right with you.
You don't have to be scared about anything,
Because we'll be here.
But if you're asking what's going to happen tomorrow,
Or,
Or, the day after that –
. . .
I just don't know.
But I do know I'll be here.

\

–   I don't really think you're a superhero Dad.
–   I know.
–   It was just a game.
–   Yeah.
–   And you don't have to play it any more.

21

– I'm a *superhero*.
– You like harassing girls?
– I was just *talking* to her. If she doesn't want to talk to
  me –
– She doesn't.
– Well if you let me go back in then I won't –
– You're not going back in.
– Hey, I'm a *superhero* –
– No one gives a shit who you think you are –
– I don't *think* anything. I *am*. I *am*.
– You're going home.
– Hey –
– Go home –
– I'm a superhero, you don't talk to superheroes that way –
– Walk away.
– Hey. Heyheyhey –
– Walk away or we'll fall out, alright?
– Come on.

Let's not get – UGH –
– What did I say? What did I say to you?
– You don't want to do that again. I don't want to have
    to hurt y-UGH –
– What did I *tell* you?
– I don't want to – UGH –
– You don't w – UGH –
****
****
******
*****
****
***
**
*

– . . .
  . . .
  . . .
  . . .
  . . .

– Yes.
  Yes.
  Yes.

– Are you
    Are you
        Are you
– Are you listening to me?
– Of course.

  What?

–   Of course.
      . . .
–   I think I need to spend some time.
      Away.
      . . .
      I need to not be here for a while.
      In this house.
      Can you understand that?
      Are you listening to me?
      Can you understand why I need to do that?

–   Of course.
      Of course I do.

–   Not for ever.
–   No.
–   But just –
–   It's fine.
–   And you'll be alright?
–   Yes.
–   . . .
–   . . .
–   I'll let you know.
      Wherever I end up, and you can call me.
      If anything –
      You can just call me.
      . . .
      Promise you'll do that.
–   Captain Amazing!
–   Promise you'll call me if you need to –
–   Captain Amazing we need your help!
–   Are you listening to me?
–   Yes. Course. Of course I will –
–   Captain Amazing we need you! There's an emergency!
–   *Mark.*
–   . . .
–   I'm leaving now, alright?
–   Okay.

Have a –
Good trip.
. . .
. . .

. . .

– Captain Amazing!
– What?
– There's an emergency!
– The old mill's on fire! There's people trapped inside!
– I'm, uh –
What's this now?
– I drew this.
– Captain Amazing! Help!
– I'm coming – I – This is a good drawing –

The train's headed straight for the cliff!

– Hang on –

I like Spider-Man best.

Men can be nurses as well.

I fell asleep.

I was sick on your coat.

– That's alright –

I was sick on Mum's bed.

– Quickly, grab on to me-

The brakes won't work! She won't stop, Captain!

My tummy's bad.

My baby! My baby's in there!

I fell down again.

–   There's so much smoke . . .

So you wear the cape all day?

–   I can wear what I want –

It's a cape?

It's kind of dirty.

You can't sleep here, sir.

You should consider some sort of spandex.

How long?

How long now?

And for saving the lives of hundreds of our town's
    steelworkers, I award you the key to the city –

–   Thank you-

When can I go back to school?

Speech Captain! Speech!

When can we go home?

Are you okay?

–   It's a great honour to receive this –

This is a very stupid thing to be doing, sir.

And then this lace goes through here . . .

–   Sometimes I feel like there's speech bubbles hanging
         over me –

We'll talk to the doctor.

–   It's all just a part of my job.

That's a good one.

That's me.

And that's Mum.

I drew your head too big.

And too bald.

Sir –

The other girls think I'm weird.

Sir, put that down –

Mark –

Mark –

–   I couldn't afford a big – It's still a diamond. It's a proper
         ring.

Stop that.

Don't touch that.

That's dirty, sweetheart –

Sir!

What did I just say?

Dog

Hat

Shoes

You can't just put on a cape and go around hitting
people –

Okay

It'll grow back. They said it'll grow back.

Okay

Get *out* –

– I'm just starting to feel like everything's overlapping
a bit –

Can I try coffee?

Can I try beer?

Can I try wine?

– I don't –

Can we get a dog?

I don't like cats.

Fuck you.

Captain Amazing, he's getting away!

– What?

Stop it.

Stop.

That's *enough*.

He's getting *away*!

Get *out* –

Dad –

– Please –

Dad –

I'll be gone anyway –

Stop that.

I could spin right round the world backwards –

I know –

Fast enough to put time back to dinosaurs –

I know –

I *know* –

Interfering with time is against the superhero code.

–   Fuck you. *Fuck you* –

Sir –

Go home.

You can't be here –

Go *home*.

Even without you writing the stories –

–   This is enough.

He'll still be flying around.

–   This is enough now-

He'll still be having adventures –

–   Please . . .

It's a *cape*.

It's a *CAPE*.

. . .

. . .

. . .

If you give me some idea of the kind of service you'd
   like –

. . .

. . .

Your ice cream is melting.

I know this is a very difficult process.

–   Do you?

Your ice cream is melting.

. . .

. . .

Don't be sad about me

. . .

. . .

. . .

Superheroes . . .

. . .

all need a reason to put on the cape.

. . .

. . .

. . .

—   . . .

. . .*flying* . . .
. . .
is a lot harder than it looks.

Some idiot once said all you needed was a happy
    thought but that's not enough.
It's a lot more work than that.
A lot harder.
It's a,
. . .
It's a very −
internal thing,
flight.

You've got to spend a lot of time in your head.
Get used to *living* in here.

Find yourself a nice, wide open space.
A field, or a, a,
. . .
A car park.
Don't worry about the cape for now, that's all just icing.
Stretch off, warm up.
That's important.
Pick a take-off spot.
Don't look straight up in the air, focus just ahead of you,
    relax –
and concentrate on lifting off.

Clear your mind –
Take a breath –
Think *positive*.
And just let go of everything that's tying you to the
    ground.

Even a centimetre at first,
That's an achievement.
Soon you'll be hovering just above the blades of grass.

Practice.

Then try a bit higher.

A bit higher.

Soon you'll be cutting through the air with ease.

It's a long process,
It'll take practice,
But it's worth it.
Flying over the pyramids at night –

Weaving through the rainforests –
The magic of it never fades.
It never gets old.

Every night I take off –
Pushing myself away from the ground,
My house,
My street,
My town,
This country.
Breaking through clouds as I go,
Watching the stars get closer.

I like to glide across the night sky,
Look down at the lights that string the globe,
The glow of the moon in the black sheets of the oceans,

Feel the world and everything in it turning beneath me.

And every night I have the same thought –

I don't know what I'd do without this.

He smiles.

Black.

The Amazing Origins of *Captain Amazing*!
or, How We Done What We Did

After I graduated from university, I spent about four years working on the fringe while working part time variously at a pub, a takeaway, and then an art gallery. The unstoppable Lucy Oliver-Harrison was my producer, and the handsome Clive Judd was my frequent director.

One day in 2009, I called Clive up to let him know I'd worked out what I wanted to do next: I was going to write an hour's worth of observational stand-up material about being a superhero and I was going to perform it myself at nightclubs while pissed. I was very into Eric Bogosian at the time (still am), and this is probably why I felt such a performance would be really exciting and edgy.

It's a testament to either how nice Clive is, or just that he was as naive as I was back then, that he also decided this was a good idea, and that we should definitely do this. Maybe he just wanted to see me get beaten up by an angry crowd. But luckily for me and all of our potential audiences, we didn't get round to it as other shows and opportunities came up.

The idea resurfaced years later, after we'd both spent a lot of time working with another friend from university, Mark Weinman, who had developed into a stunning actor.

'Why don't we get Mark to do that *Captain Amazing* idea you had?' said Clive, probably, in my memory.

'But aren't I going to perform that one day?' I blustered.

Clive went silent. (Probably.)

So instead, I ran the idea past Mark and he loved it. By now I'd developed the story: it was still a piece of stand-up comedy, but the engine that drove it along was an unspoken tragedy that had caused this man to go and humiliate himself night after night in comedy clubs either as a kind of self-flagellation, or just as a way to be heard by someone. It was now becoming, as my mum likes to call them, one of my 'miserable plays'.

But the play went on the backburner for a few years as by this point the three of us were all busy doing other things – Clive and Mark were very in demand with various theatres, and I was getting really into *Battlestar Galactica*, so we all had things going on.

What most likely kicked it into action again was a monologue of mine called *Mr Noodles* that Mark performed on Halloween 2011, which was about a shy and introverted office worker who meets a violent psychopathic talking dog who convinces him to abandon all his inhibitions and give in to his animal side. It was a comedy. But the reason it was the stepping stone to *Captain Amazing* was the form: although a lot of the text was direct address to audience, there were several long passages where Mark would play the office worker and the eponymous dog and have a series of back-and-forth exchanges. Very few actors could pull this off convincingly, but Mark's energy and attack made the stage feel as though it was populated by more than one actor, and he made the play sing with life and power (I should also mention he was aided by brilliant direction from the brilliant Ned Bennett).

By this point, I had struck up a relationship with Live Theatre in Newcastle, who were considering one or two of my other plays. Once a year they, along with The Empty Space, give funds to writers, directors or artists to come to the Theatre and develop a piece of work, and the launch of this coincided with Mark and I starting to talk about the Captain again.

At the pitch meeting, I told them that we were intending to write material and then have Mark actually go and test-drive it at real open-mic nights across Newcastle, in character and in costume. This was almost certainly the main reason we were awarded the money, and it was also something I just said on the spot, and hadn't run it past Mark even once.

Luckily for him, when I actually sat down to write the thing, the stand-up format wasn't working. I wrote a huge amount of material but it didn't feel right at all – it was too on-the-nose, it was too gimmicky and, crucially, it wasn't funny.

What I *did* like were the few small exchanges I'd written between the Captain and his daughter, whom I'd christened Emily. I loved her immediately, and I loved how the two of them were struggling through conversations about the world together, so I set aside all the material I'd written prior to this, and just started writing pages and pages of their conversations.

This is very different from how I normally write; it was a much looser, throwing-a-lot-of-things-at-the-wall process, but it felt right as I started compiling all these fractured little moments from their relationship. It became very clear that this was where the real story was, and that this was the form. And as the form shifted, so did the story: the real heart of the play was now about an emotionally crippled man forced into articulacy by the arrival of his daughter. The creation of a superhero bedtime story enables him to communicate with her in ways he finds impossible otherwise, and this new-found freedom in fantasy soon starts to seep into other areas of his life too.

Content and form suddenly came together much more clearly, and I decided the whole play had to be written like this, like those exchanges I had started writing for *Mr Noodles*: the story would be written just like a normal, multi-character play, but only performed by one actor. It was a memory play, and it was also a sort of children's play for adults, like a bedtime story where your mum or dad would do all the different voices of the characters for you. It was also a sparse, open text, and while developing it at Live Theatre with Mark, almost every alteration I made was a cut rather than an addition. I wanted the text to be something for the actor to springboard from, to provide as many opportunities as possible for interesting and intimate moments with the audience. It was an actor's play, through and through.

After the development there were a lot of other projects getting juggled, so ultimately *Captain Amazing* didn't open until

April 2013, in a sort-of mini-season with another of my plays, *Brilliant Adventures* (I hope one day to write a play with 'Fantastic' in the title to complete a triptych of enthusiastic titles). Clive finally got to direct it in a wonderfully clear and crisp production, and it was supported by beautiful illustrations by Rebecca Glover, which helped Mark to paint a vivid imaginary world for the characters. As a result of him being with me throughout the development, the text was custom-fitted for him, and his performance was extraordinary. He was magical and ultimately shattering, and he elevated my text into something almost mythic in quality and tone, for which I'll forever be grateful. I also have to give a mention to the fantastic Gez Casey at Live Theatre, who was the real champion of the play, and without him I doubt we'd have gotten here.

So that's how we got to this point – I hope you enjoy/enjoyed the show, or if you're just reading this as a script, I hope you enjoy/enjoyed that too. Thank you for supporting new writing for the theatre, and thank you for allowing me the pleasure and privilege of telling you a story.

Alistair McDowall, 2014

Talk Show

.

for dad and grandad

Talk Show was first performed in the Jerwood Downstairs Space at the Royal Court Theatre, London, as part of the Open Court season, on 16 July 2013, with the following cast and creatives:

Sam	Ryan Sampson
Bill	Ferdy Roberts
Jonah	Jonjo O'Neill
Ron	Alan Williams
Darryl	Nav Sidhu
Steve	Lee Armstrong

Director   Caroline Steinbeis
Designer   Chloe Lamford
Composer / Sound Designer   Nick Powell and Giles Thomas
Lighting Designer   Lizzie Powell

Characters

Sam, *twenty-six, nervy*
Bill, *early fifties, broad shoulders*
Jonah, *early thirties, skeletal*
Ron, *eighties, quick*
Darryl, *late twenties*
Steve, *early twenties*

Place

A small market town in the North-East of England

Time

2012

Notes

No strong accents.

A question without a question mark denotes a flatness of tone.

A dash (–) indicates an interruption of speech or train of thought.

An ellipsis (. . .) indicates either a trailing off, a breather, a shift, or a transition.

A slash (/) indicates where the next line of dialogue interrupts or overlaps.

1.

We're in a half-converted basement in a small house.
A rickety staircase against the back wall leading upstairs.
Small window high up on the stage right wall.
A small bed beneath the window, scuff marks on the wall above it.
A stained rug, and a few pictures and posters tacked to the walls.
There are stacks and stacks of books against walls and on the stairs.

Every piece of furniture in the room seems to be broken or torn and held together with tape, and in small heaps around the room are empty beer cans and filthy clothes.

In the middle of the room, a tired sofa and a cheap desk are arranged in the manner of a late-night talk show.
Behind them, a red curtain hides the space beneath the staircase.
We can see the legs of someone sitting at the top of the stairs.
Two cameras are stood on cheap tripods, sitting just in front of the audience, pointed at the set-up.
Cables run from them to a laptop under the desk.

After a moment, a jaunty theme kicks in.

Sam (*off/amplified*)   Live! From his dad's basement, it's The Sam Starling Show!

Recorded applause is heard.

(*Off/amplified.*) The *only* late night talk show operating in the North-East!
And now, since there's no alternative, here's Sam!

Canned applause and cheering.

Sam *emerges from behind his red curtain and stumbles forward in front of his desk.*
He's wearing a cheap suit.

Thank you, thank you.
Please –

Thank you –
Please, we're pushing for time.
If you like, you can all stay behind and applaud me afterwards.

Canned laughter.

So let's get on with it –
In the news today a man in Scotland claims his *cat* is possessed
by the spirit of his dead wife.
Did you read about this?
Apparently he only realised this after he'd been caught in bed
with it.

Laughter.

You know, if I *had* writers, I'd fire them for that one.

Laughter.

Children from schools in our district made the local papers
this week after a world record attempt for the largest recorder
choir.
Six headteachers were later arrested and escorted to The
Hague for crimes against humanity.

Laughter.

Incidentally, I called up the world records people this week –
I wanted to see if I could qualify for 'least watched talk show' –

Laughter.

But apparently there's a minimum number of audience
members needed to qualify as a *show*, and I was informed that
technically what I'm broadcasting here is just an unanswered
cry for help.

Laughter, applause.

And finally – Come on, don't applaud that –
Finally, the local council have made a desperate bid to
stimulate growth in the town centre by drastically lowering
rent for store-owners.

I once tried to stimulate growth in town myself, but was quickly arrested for indecent exposure.

Laughter, applause.

A cheap one to end us on there –
We've got a wonderful show for you, so let's get to it –
You'll know tonight's guest as the assistant manager of Tasty Chicken on Cross Street. He's a local boy running a local business, please give a warm welcome to Darryl Seymour!

Applause, music.

Darryl *comes down the stairs, looking mystified.*

Sam *shakes his hand and gestures for him to sit down, before taking his place behind the desk and picking up his cards.*

Sam   Darryl, great to see you, thanks for stopping by.

Darryl   Uh, okay.

Sam   You got my message about formal attire?

Laughter.

This is your uniform I take it?

Darryl   Yeah, we're open Mond –

Sam   Doesn't Darryl look great tonight, ladies and gents?

Applause.

They come for the fried chicken and stay for the hunk behind the counter.

Laughter.

Were you working today?

Darryl   I'm supposed to be there now.

Sam   But the call of celebrity was too great.

Darryl   My dad said I had to do this. For the free advertising. I didn't want to.

Beat.

Laughter.

Sam   Well we appreciate your honesty, Darryl.

Laughter.

Now Darryl, there's one thing I'm sure we're all desperate to know –
I want you to know you can trust me with this –
What is your chicken actually *made* of?

Laughter.

Darryl   It's just chicken.

Sam   Come on. Darryl. You can trust me.
What percentage is newspaper and sawdust?

Laughter.

Darryl   It's chicken.

Sam   Darryl –

Darryl (*standing*)   I don't think I can be arsed with this –

Sam   Wai – Alright – Okay –
Uh –

Beat.

Sam   So Darryl, Tasty Chicken's on Cross Street, and –

Darryl   We open Monday to Saturdays 11 a.m. till 4 a.m.
and Sundays 12 p.m. till midnight.

Sam   Yes. And, ah –

Darryl   Free wings with every four-piece meal.

Beat.

Sam   Okay.
. . .
Do you, do you work long hours?

Darryl   Pretty long.

Sam   But it's a rewarding job?

Darryl   I get paid.

Pause.

Sam *scratches his head.*

Sam   Uh – So Darryl, we hear you have an amusing anecdote about Tasty Chicken.

Darryl   Shall I do it now?

Sam   I think we'd all love to hear it?

Applause.

Darryl   So – Well –
One night it's pretty busy and these two lads are starting some trouble with each other, squaring up to each other and that –

Sam   Were they fighting over your chicken?

Laughter.

Darryl   No they were just fucking around.
And I'm telling them to take it outside,
And we keep a baseball bat under the counter –

Sam   That's something we have in common.

Laughter.

Darryl   So they go outside and start scrapping, and everyone's watching, and then one of em throws a punch, and either he's wearing a ring or he just hits at the right angle because the other guy's eye just bursts.

Beat.

Sam   He –

Darryl   His eye just pops in his fucking skull.
. . .
That's my story.

Pause.

Sam   Well Darryl, I'm not sure if that's a *funny* story, but it's definitely a story.

Laughter, applause.

Fade out.

Fade in, later, applause and cheering. **Sam** *shouts over it.*

Sam   And thank you to our guest, Darryl Seymour from Tasty Chicken!

Cheering.

And to you all for watching. We'll be back on Monday night, have a great weekend and we look forward to seeing you then. Good night!

The music starts up.
Sam *shakes* **Darryl***'s hand and then goes around to the front of the desk waving to the 'audience'.*

The music ends.

Sam   That's it.

Darryl   That's it?

Sam   That's it.

Darryl   You said it was funny.

Sam   Well, it's kind of a –

Darryl   It wasn't.

Sam   Okay.

Darryl   You're not funny.

Sam   It's more of a –

Darryl   You're not funny.

Sam   Well, you know, your funny story was more of a horrific incident if we're being –

Darryl   You said to bring a story.

Sam   Like a humorous kind of a – Not a violent episode.

Darryl   You said bring a story.

Sam   Well thanks, you know – Thank you for your eye-gouging story.

Darryl   How many watch this?

Sam   It's, it's in the high hundreds.

Darryl   You said thousands.

Sam   I think hundreds is pretty good.

Darryl   You said thousands.
You said all over the world on the internet people were watching this.

Sam   People watch. People were watching.

Darryl   That's the only reason my dad made me do this. You said we'd be idiots not to.

Sam   I stand by that.

Darryl   You said you're a local celebrity. All kinds of people watch –

Sam   I'm a – It's good for business, I promise.

Darryl   I've never heard of you.

Sam   It's kind of a select –

Darryl   I've never heard of you.

Sam   All my other guests have experienced some kind of a, a –
An *upswing*. In their businesses.

Darryl   What other guests?

Sam   All kinds of people – If you *watched* the show, you'd know.
You could get it hooked up on your big screen so your customers can watch.

Darryl   We play music in the shop.

Sam   I'll come do it for you. Maybe if they watch me they won't burst each other's eyes. I'm a, a very calming influence.

Darryl   My dad told you to talk about how good our food is.

Sam   Well, you know, I can't *lie* to people –

Darryl   What?

Sam   Your food tastes like you found it round the back of a hospital.

Darryl *punches* **Sam** *in the stomach.*

Darryl   You're a fucking loser.

Sam   . . . maybe . . .

Darryl   What's the point of this?

He heads to go.

Sam   Wait can you –
Can you go out the window?

Darryl   The window.

Sam *opens the window.*

Sam   My dad sleeps in the front room, and it's late –

Darryl   I'll be quiet.

Sam   No, I mean, he's – His bed is right by the door. I promised we wouldn't go up there.
. . .
Please don't hit me again.

Beat.

Darryl   Fucking hell . . .

He heads over to the bed.

I just –

Sam   Don't mind your shoes, just climb up –

Darryl *does.*

Sam   There you –
Go –
Thanks for coming, spread the word!

Darryl (*off*)   You're a prick.

Sam *starts taking his suit off.*

Sam   Yeah, probably.

He lifts his shirt and looks at his stomach.

Definitely.

He goes over and looks at the laptop.
Clicks about.
He's now stripped down to his boxers.
He hums.

He goes behind the curtain and comes back with a beer.
He snaps it open and drinks as he hangs his suit up.

Jonah's *face appears at the window, unnoticed.*

He disappears again just as quick.

Sam *goes over to the cameras and turns them off, still humming.*

He starts singing something, occasionally swapping words for whatever
he's doing.

Through the open window, **Jonah** *leaps in and lands with a thud.*
Barefoot, stripped to the waist.
He is covered in dust and ash and sand and dirt and dried blood.
His button fly is done up wrong.

Sam *yelps.*

Beat.

Jonah *approaches* **Sam***,*
who backs away in a panic.

Sam   Waitwaitwaitjesusfuckdon't –
I don't have any money –

Jonah *rests his hands on* **Sam**'s *shoulders.*

Jonah   Sammy.

Sam   Oh –
Jonah –
Shit –
I didn't –
I thought you were –

Jonah   I've come back.

Sam   We're naked . . .

Jonah   How are you?

Sam   I, I,

Jonah   What's wrong?

Sam   Sorry, you just –

Jonah   I scare you?

Sam   A little bit, a little –

Jonah   You're shaky.

Sam   Your entrance –
I thought you were some kind of –
What happened to your clothes?

Jonah   How old are you?

Sam   How –

Jonah   How old are you?

Sam   Twenty-six.

Jonah   Twenty-six . . .

*He smooshes **Sam**'s face.*

Sam   That's my . . . age.

Jonah   You look good.

Sam   You look –

Jonah   I look bad?

Sam   You're . . . dusty.

He sits down, catches himself.

Jonah   I couldn't find the house, I couldn't remember which
house it was.
I don't go indoors often.
I was walking around and I went in gardens and some house I
thought was the house, but it wasn't, and that didn't go down
well but then I remembered the basement.
So I looked for houses with basements and this is the only one.

Sam   It's the only basement . . .

Jonah   It's strange to have a basement here.
Who was that?

Sam   What?

Jonah   Climbed out the window.
He your friend?

Sam   No, he's just some . . .
Guy.

Jonah   Are you alright?

Sam   Yeah, I just −

He wrestles into a T-shirt he grabs off the floor.

Jonah   Are you happy to see me?

Sam   Course − Course I am − It's just a shock −

Jonah   I should've come in the front?

Sam   Maybe − I −

Jonah   It was late.
I heard you talking down here.

Sam   Yes −

Jonah   I didn't want to wake people up.

Sam   I know, I just haven't seen you for −

Jonah   Is this where you sleep?

Sam   I – Yes –

Jonah   This your bed, here?

Sam   Yes.

Jonah   You have three pillows, you like to use three pillows?

Sam   I don't –

Jonah   You have a toilet?

Sam   Not –
We can't go upstairs. Dad's asleep in the front.

Jonah   He sleeps in the front room?

Sam *nods.*

Jonah   Liz makes him sleep on the sofa?

Sam   They – Split up.

Beat.

Jonah   They're divorced?

Sam *nods.*

Jonah   Your mum's gone?

Sam   Not *gone*, but –

Jonah   When?

Sam   A while ago. Years. I don't –
What are you doing here?

Beat.

Sam   I'm sorry –
You've been –
Gone.

. . .

A really long time.

It's kind of a surprise to *see* you, just –
Out of the blue.
You just jumped in through my window, half dressed and –
I don't mean to,
Narrate you, but –
You did.

Pause.

Jonah *stares.*

Jonah   Your hair's different.

Sam   My – Hair?

Jonah   It's different. It's longer.
It's very stylish.
Is it?

Sam   I don't know –

Jonah   Mine used to be long.
I had very long hair for a while. I had it tied back, but then
I got lice.
My head was crawling with lice, big ones, the size of buttons
and rocks –
I went into a barbers and I stole the shaving – the – what do
you call them?

Sam   Clippers?

Jonah   Clippers, yeah, and I had to get it all off.
Because of the lice.
. . .
It's grown a bit now.

Pause.

Why's he sleep in the front?

Sam   He – Grandad's in his room.

Jonah   Dad's in his room?

Sam   Yeah.

Jonah   He lives here now?

Sam   Yeah.

Jonah   Why?

Sam   He kept . . . falling over at home and hurting himself so Dad moved him here.

Jonah   Why was he falling over?

Sam   I don't –

Jonah   Is he sick?

Sam   No.
He's just old.

Pause.

Jonah   You sold the house?

Sam   It – It was a rental.

Jonah   It was not.

Sam   It was.

Jonah   Dad owns his house.

Sam   He did, but then he sold it and moved to a rental.
. . .
And now he's here.

Pause.

Jonah   Hm.

Pause.

Sam   What are you doing here?

Jonah   What.

Sam   Why are you –

Jonah   I'm allowed.

Sam   I'm not saying – Just – Are you here to –
To like – To live . . .

Jonah   I don't know, I've just come back. I'm back now.
I need to stay here.

Sam   I don't know if that'll –

Jonah   I need to stay here, I'm family.

Beat.

I've come back.

Beat.

Sam   Won't Dad –

Jonah   Don't tell your dad.

Sam   I can't just –

Jonah   Don't tell your dad.
Or my dad.
Don't tell your dad or my dad.

Sam   Why?

Jonah   Because.

Beat.

Don't tell them.

Sam   But how will you –

Jonah   I'll be gone in the day.
Just put me up at night.
They won't know.
I'll use the window.
Don't tell them.
Promise.

Beat.

Sam   This is –

Jonah   Promise.

Sam   *Okay.*
But just don't –

Jonah   I have to piss.
Go outside?

Sam   No, there's –
There's some bottles back there –

Jonah   You piss in these bottles?

Sam   They're screwcapped.
They don't smell.

Jonah   I just piss in one right here?

Sam   Just don't spill.

Jonah *grabs one of the bottles and goes to a corner to piss.*

Beat.

Sam   You probably can't –

Jonah   I'm going.

Sam   Sorry.

Pause.

Jonah *screws the lid on the bottle.*
He sniffs it.

Jonah   You throw these out?

Sam   I don't *keep* them.

Jonah   Where do you shit?

Sam   I hold it in.

Jonah   You shit in the mornings?

Sam   Yeah – Jonah –

Jonah *pulls a tobacco pouch out from the crotch of his pants and starts rolling a cigarette.*

Jonah   What?

Sam   You probably shouldn't stay more than the weekend –

Jonah   Why?

He is going through **Sam***'s stuff as he rolls his cigarette.*
He uses his feet.

Sam   Just because –
It won't be very convenient –

Jonah   Con*venient*.

Sam   There are obviously – *issues* that –

Jonah   Your music is old.

Sam   Will you listen?

Jonah   You don't have new music.

Sam   They're mostly Mum's.

Jonah   You're young, you want young people music.

Sam   I'm not that young.

Jonah   You're young.
You're young.
. . .
You've got nothing to play em on.

Sam   Dad sold the stereo.

Jonah   He sold your stereo?

Sam   He sells everything.

Jonah   He sells your stuff?

Sam   He needs the money.

Jonah   Why?

Sam   He lost his job.

Jonah   The lumber yard job?

Sam   It shut.

Jonah   The wood place shut down?

Sam   They weren't making money, so first they tried to fire him, but he said he'd take a pay cut, and then they had to shut down anyway.

Jonah   So he's got no job?

Sam   Uh-uh.

Jonah   What's your job?

Sam   I don't have one.

Jonah   You worked at the video shop –

Sam   It shut. Everything's shut.

Jonah   So he sells your stuff.

Sam   He sells all our stuff.
He sold the washing machine.

Jonah   He sold the washing machine?

Sam   We go to the laundrette.

Jonah   He's not had a job a long time?

Sam   Sometimes the job centre makes him work for free at other places.

Jonah   Where?

Sam   He had to go work at a supermarket and they made him do all the worst jobs.
Everyone else there was a teenager.

Jonah (*smiles*)   Really?

Sam   It's not funny.

A baby monitor on the desk sputters into life.
Jonah *leaps back.*

Bill (*baby monitor*)   Quiet down there, it's late.

Beat.

Jonah *looks to* **Sam**.

Sam   It's so he can tell me to shut up without coming downstairs.

Jonah   Can he hear me?

Sam   It's a baby monitor. It's like, one-way.

Jonah *looks at it.*

Sam   How long do you think you need to stay?

Jonah   What is this?
What's this curtain?

Sam   You're asking so many questions . . .

Jonah   What is it?

Sam   It's my . . . hobby.

Jonah   What's your hobby?

Beat.

What?

Sam   I don't –

Jonah   Tell me.

Pause.

Sam   I –
Have a talk show.
. . .

Beat.

Jonah   You have a talk show.

Sam   I have an . . . internet talk show.

Jonah   You have a talk show that goes on the internet.

Sam   Yes.

Jonah   And you make it.

Sam   Yeah.

Jonah   You do the questions and you have guests and it goes on the internet.

Sam *nods.*

Beat.

Jonah   People watch it?

Sam   Some people.

Jonah   Who watches it?

Sam   People. People do.

Jonah   Who do you talk to?

Sam   All kinds of . . .
Local business people.
Or artists.
Local bands and stuff.

Jonah   You do it Friday nights?

Sam   I do it every night.

Jonah   *Every* night?

Sam   Weeknights. Which is why you can't –

Jonah   You sit here with these cameras and talk to people and make jokes and put it on the internet.

Sam   Yeah.

Jonah   Like Parkinson.

Sam   More like –
Johnny Carson.

Jonah   Who?

Sam   He's kind of my, uh –
Or David Letterman, or, you know –

Jonah   Who?

Sam   Americans. Like the American style of –
It's just a hobby.

Jonah   You don't have an audience?

Sam   I have like a –
I have a remote that makes my laptop –
It plays laughter and applause and the theme tune and stuff.
I do all the sound effects with this clicker.

Jonah   You can't get a friend to do that?

Sam   I, I can do it myself.

Pause.

What?

Jonah   You do this.

Sam   Yeah.

Jonah   You have all the confidence and stuff you need to do this.

Sam   I'm okay.

Jonah   And people watch it?

Sam   On the internet, yeah.

Jonah   You're funny?

Sam   I – I'm trying.

Jonah   Why?

Sam   What?

Jonah   Why do you do it?

Sam   I just . . .
I just do.
. . .
Gotta do something.

Pause.

Jonah *smiles.*

Sam   What?

*He ruffles **Sam**'s hair.*

Sam   I'm pretty tired, Jonah.

Jonah   Do you need to sleep?

Sam   It's late.

Jonah   I could sleep.

He goes over to the sofa and lies down.
*He finds **Sam**'s beer on the way and takes it with him.*
He lies on the sofa.
Smokes, drinks.
A moment.

Sam   So,
You can stay the weekend,
cos I don't do the show weekends,
but,
you know –

Jonah   I won't get in the way.

Beat.

Sam   Kay.

He grabs his toothbrush and a bottle of water from his bed and brushes his teeth.

Jonah *stares at the ceiling.*

Sam *spits out the window and closes it.*

Beat.

Night.

He turns the light off, gets into bed.

Pause.

Jonah   You should have me on your show.

Sam   Maybe.

Jonah   I got some stories.

Sam   I bet.

Pause.

Sam   You're not gonna – You and Dad aren't gonna fight or anything, are you?

Jonah   Don't tell your dad I'm here.

Sam I, I won't, but –

Jonah   Or my dad.

Sam   I won't tell anyone.

Jonah   Good.

Pause.

Jonah   Have a girlfriend?

Sam   No.

Jonah   Why not?

Sam   I just –
Don't.
. . .
You talk weird.

Jonah   I haven't talked to anyone for a while.
. . .
Get better.

Pause.

Sam   Jonah?

Jonah   What?

Sam   Where've you been?

Pause.

Jonah   I've just been away.

Beat.

Sam   Are you alright?

Beat.

Jonah   I've come back now.

Fade.

2.

The same.
Sam *is woken by* **Bill** *pouring a glass of water on his face.*

Sam Guh –

Bill Get up.

Sam Why would you do that?

Bill I was shouting you.

Sam You –

He suddenly scans the room.

Bill What?

Sam N –
Nothing.

Bill It smells awful down here.
What is it?

Sam I don't know – / I'm wet.

Bill Smells like a gutter.

He opens the window.

Sam You're borrowing my suit.

Bill It's a shared suit.

Sam It's my suit, it doesn't even fit you.
It's like a size too small.

Bill It's fine.

Sam You look like a mod.

Bill You're taking your grandad to the clinic.

Sam You look like you've been through the wash.

Bill Yes?

Sam Yes, okay. I am.

Beat.

Bill   You wet?

Sam   Course I'm wet, you just poured water on me. That's what wet is.

Bill   I need to talk to you.

Sam   What?

Beat.

Bill *sits down on the arm of the sofa.*
His trousers crawl up his legs.

Bill   I'm –

Sam   It's really too small.

Bill   I'm trying to talk to you –

Sam   What job is it?

Bill   It's an off-licence. Night shifts.

Sam   Like an all-night off-licence.

Bill   Yes.

Sam   Kwik Booze?

Bill   Yes.

Sam   So you'll be in that sort-of cage?

Bill   I guess so.

Sam   And you need a suit for that?

Bill   It's a job interview, you wear a suit for a job interview. You'd know that if you ever went for one.

Sam   I've been to job interviews.

Bill   Listen.

Sam   I went to one last week.

Bill   Sam.

. . .

I'm going to try and sell the house.

Pause.

Sam   This house?

Bill   Course this house, what other house?

Sam   You're going to sell it?

Bill   I think we should – Rent something, something more in our –

Sam   You can't sell the house.

Bill   Sam –

Sam   Dad, you can't sell the house, it's your only asset.

Bill   It's an asset because you can sell it, and we need to sell it.

Sam   But –

Bill   The way things are –
It's sell now, or be kicked out later.

Pause.

Okay?

Beat.

Sam   No one'll want to buy it anyway.

Bill   Someone will.

Sam   Who would want this house?

Bill   Someone will.

Beat.

It's a good idea.

Sam   What about Mum?

Bill   I spoke to your mum, she agrees.

Sam   You have to split it with her?

Bill   She's letting me have whatever we get as a loan.

Sam   A loan?

Bill   Sam, I don't know how many times I can tell you this –
We have no fucking money.
Alright?
. . .

Sam   I've been trying to –

Bill   Okay –

Sam   There's nothing here –

Bill   Then maybe you shouldn't be here.

Beat.

There's no reason for you to stay here.

Beat.

No job, no friends –

Sam   I have my show –

Bill   A hobby.

Sam   It's not a hobby –

Bill   And the internet's getting cut off next week, so you'll
need a new hobby.

Sam   What?

Bill   It's going.

Sam   It's barely –

Bill   Sam, if you find me the money, I'll pay it.
You're the only one who uses it –

Sam   Grandad uses it –

Bill   Grandad looks at bird-watching pages. We can get him
a book.

Sam   We could use eBay to sell some stuff –

Bill   We don't have much left to sell.

Beat.

It's not an essential. Sorry.

He gets up and starts for the stairs.

Don't be late for the doctor –

He spots the records.
Goes over and rifles through them.

You think these are worth anything?

Sam   Most of those are Mum's.

Bill   She won't mind.
Will that record shop take them?

Sam   Maybe – I don't –
Can I keep one please?

Bill   We sold the stereo –

Sam   I just want to keep one.

Beat.

Bill *offers the records.*
Sam *plucks one out.*

Sam   Thank you.

Bill   Alright.
. . .

He gestures with the records.

I'll get us something good for tea.

He heads back upstairs.

Pause.

We hear the front door slam.

Jonah *emerges from behind the curtain in his underpants.*

Jonah   He came down for the suit.
I went behind the curtain.
He took your records.

Sam   They're Mum's.

Jonah   Him and her still friendly?

Sam   Yeah.

Jonah   She have a boyfriend?

Sam   She has a husband.

He starts getting dressed.

Jonah   She's married again?

Sam   Yeah.

Jonah   Is he good?

Sam   He's fine. He's nice.

Jonah   Do you see them much?

Sam   All the time.
We have to borrow money off them all the time.

Jonah   And Billy doesn't have a new –

Sam   Course not.

Beat.

Jonah *nods.*

Sam   Jonah –

Jonah   I can get you the money.

Sam   What?

Jonah   For the internet, so you can do your show.
He said he couldn't pay the bill. That means your show stops.

Sam   Yeah, but –

Beat.

It's not important, really –

Jonah   I think it is.
I think it's extremely important.
I get it.

Beat.

Sam   I –

Jonah   I get it. It's important.
I'll get you the money.

Sam   You don't need to do that.

Jonah   I'm your uncle.
I'm supposed to do things for you.
It'll be like rent.
Rent money for you.
I'll get you it. Don't worry.

Sam   Jonah, that's not – Maybe you and Dad should –

Jonah   I need a shower.
And some clothes.

Ron (*from off*)   Sam!

Ron*'s legs appear at the top of the stairs.*
Jonah *ducks out of sight.*

Sam   Yeah?

Ron   I'm making some bacon, do you want some bacon?

Sam   No th –

Jonah *gestures frantically.*

Sam   Actually, that'd be good, please.

Ron   Well will you give me a hand, I can't work the what's-it-called . . .

Ron's *legs disappear.*

Jonah   Bring me some bacon.

Sam   Alright.

Jonah   A lot.

Sam   I'll bring what I can.

Jonah   And a bucket of water.

Sam   What?

Jonah   A tub or something or a bucket. To wash.

Sam   Okay –
Just –

Jonah   Bring me a lot of bacon.

Sam   I'll do my best.

He hurries upstairs.

Jonah *starts rifling through the piles of clothes.*
He finds a pair of tracky bottoms that look like they'll fit, and a T-shirt.
He studies the T-shirt.

Sam *appears at the top of the stairs with a bucket of water.*
Jonah *grabs it.*

Sam   Here, quick –

Ron (*from off*)   Sam?

Sam   Coming! Soap.

He flings a bar of soap.

Jonah   Why's Abraham Lincoln on this?

Sam   What?

Jonah   Why do you have Abraham Lincoln on a shirt?

Sam   He's just –
He's my hero.

Ron (*from off*)   Sam!

Jonah   Why's he your hero?

Sam   What do you mean? The Civil –
I have to go.

He hurries off.

Jonah *looks at the shirt some more.*

He picks up his bucket and lifts it out the window,
pushing it into the yard outside.
He grabs his new clothes and pulls himself up and out the window.

Beat.

The filthy pants fly in through the window.

Beat.

Suddenly, water gushes in and on to the bed.

Pause.

Jonah *slides back in, soaking wet and dressed.*

He looks at the bed.

Enter **Sam** *with a plate of bacon.*

Sam   Here –

Jonah   I wet your bed.

Sam   What – Why?

Jonah   I was showering.

Sam   Why's everyone pouring water on my bed?

Ron (*from off*)   Sam! Stop running off!

Sam   Eat this.

He hurries off.

Jonah *sits on the sofa and eats the bacon with his hands quickly.*

He looks around the room as he eats.

He sees some shoes on the floor, holds them up against his feet.

Too big.

He rifles around, still eating bacon.

He finds some sandals.

He straps them on tightly.

He clomps about a bit.

He's finished the bacon.

He licks the plate.

Enter **Sam**.

Jonah   More?

Sam   That's it. We had one pack.

Jonah *licks the plate.*

Sam   What are you gonna do? I have to take Grandad –

Jonah   Why's he have to go to a clinic?

Sam   Just – Blood pressure stuff. Old guy stuff.
He hates going.

Jonah   You said he was fine.

Sam   He is.

Jonah   Why's he have to go then?

Sam   He just – does.

Beat.

He's fine.

Jonah   I need a book.

Sam   What?

Jonah   A book to read, I need a book.

He rifles through the books.

Sam   Just – Take whatever you – You're exhausting.

Jonah   These are all Americans.
I don't like the Americans.

Sam   They're not all Americans.

Jonah   You have any Russians?

Sam   I don't know   I don't think –

Jonah   You should get some Russians.
They know what it's all about.

Sam   What what's all about?

Jonah   Everything.
I'm taking Moby Dick.

Sam   You can keep Moby-Dick.
Are those my sandals?

Jonah   They're big.
You have bigger feet than me.
It's strange.

Pause.

He looks at them.

Jonah   See ya.

He clambers out the window.

Sam   Bye . . .

Beat.

He sighs quietly.

. . . Shit.

Fade.

3.

The same.
Dark.

We can hear a conversation, muffled, through the ceiling.

A moment.

Jonah *slips in through the window.*
He has a carrier bag.

He looks around. He takes a beer out of his bag and starts to drink.

He looks up at the ceiling and tries to hear what they're saying.

He gives up and goes and sits on the sofa.

He looks up at the ceiling again.

He spots the baby monitor on the table and turns it on.

Voices:

Ron   – and as soon as they start going to the doctors, that's it.

Bill   Don't be daft.

Ron   I'm not being daft, I'd just sooner leave things as they are.

Bill   We know –

Ron   And he says I'm perfectly capable / of looking after myself.

Bill   No one's saying –

Ron   It's a waste of everyone's time.

Bill   It's once a week. Stop moaning.

Ron   I'm not moaning, I'm just telling you what he said.

Bill   Do you want more rice?

Ron   No I don't, no thank you.

Sam   I'll have some.

Clinking of plates and cutlery.

Jonah *takes a bag of spinach out of his bag and eats.*

A long pause.

Sam   Did you get the job?

Bill   I don't know.

Sam   They didn't say –

Bill   I don't *know*, Sam.

Pause.

Sam   How do you feel about the house, Grandad?

Pause.

Ron   Well.
We do what we have to.

Bill   Exactly.

Sam   I think it's a stupid idea.

Bill   Course you do. You hate change.

Sam   We shouldn't lose another house –

Bill   Don't bring / that up.

Ron   I tried to keep you out of that.

Bill   We don't need to get into it Dad.

Ron   I just didn't want to make a fuss.

Bill   Let's not talk about it.

Pause.

Sam   What if Jonah comes back?

Pause.

What if he came back and couldn't find us.
. . .
Because we'd moved.

Pause.

Bill   I don't think we need to worry about that.

. . .

Pause.

Sam   Why not?

Bill   Why are you bringing him up?

Sam   I'm just saying –

Bill   Well don't.

. . .

Why would we want to talk about him?

Sam   He might –

Jonah *turns the monitor off.*

He stares at the ceiling.

Muffled voices.

A long pause.

He turns the monitor back on.

Silence.

He opens a beer.

Sam   You shouldn't say things like that.

. . .

He's your brother.

Bill   Let's just eat.

Fade.

4.

The same.
Later.
Still dark.
Sam *comes down the stairs, closing the door behind him.*

Sam (*quietly*)   Jonah?
. . .
Jonah?

He turns a dim lamp on.

Jonah *is lying under the desk.*

Sam   You're under the desk.

Jonah   No one calls me Jonah.
. . .

Sam   What?

Jonah   I don't tell people that's my name.
. . .
I say I'm called Jon.

Sam *squats down next to him.*

Sam   Are you alright?

Jonah   Do you know why they chose it?
My name.

Beat.

Sam   No . . .

Jonah   Me either.
There's not many.
It's me and the guy in the whale.
He got eaten by the whale?

Sam   . . . he got swallowed, but he was okay.
It spat him out.

Jonah   Cos God told him to.

Sam   He kind of –

Jonah   Why did it eat him anyway?

Sam   He, uh –

. . .

He ran away from God.

Beat.

Jonah *is listening.*

Sam   He was supposed to –
To do something, I don't remember –
But instead he got on a boat.
To run away from whatever it was God told him to do –
And obviously God noticed –
So he made this big storm, which was going to smash up the
boat and drown everyone on it –
So,
Ah,
He,
Jonah –
Told the people on the boat that God was after him,
that's why the storm was so bad,
and that they should throw him overboard.
And they did . . .
And the storm stopped.

Beat.

Jonah   And that's when the whale ate him.

Sam   Yeah, and he repented inside the whale, so God made
the whale spit him out.

Pause.

Jonah   Do you believe in God?

Sam   No.

Jonah   Me either.

Pause.

Sam   Do you want to get out from under there?

Beat.

Jonah *stands up.*

Sam   You can have my bed.

Jonah   I'm fine.

Sam   We'll take turns.

He leads **Jonah** *over to the bed.* **Jonah** *gets in, fully clothed.*

Sam   There you go.

Jonah   Why do you still care about me.

Sam   Why do I still *care* about you?

Beat.

Jonah   I hit you that time.
Knocked you out.
Split your lip.

Sam   Yeah, but . . .
. . .
You also taught me how to ride a bike.
. . .
So it balances out I guess.

Pause.

Jonah *stares at the ceiling.*

Sam *sits on the sofa.*

A long pause.

Jonah   Do they talk about Mum much?
My mum.

Beat.

Sam   No.
Not really.
They don't talk about anything much.

Jonah   You should have them on your show.

Sam (*smiles*)   Yeah.

Jonah   You should put me on your show.

Pause.

I wasn't there.
For Mum.

. . .
Two funerals in a year . . .
You know.

. . .
Was it good?

Sam   It was a funeral.

Jonah   Was it nice. Was it how she'd want it.

Sam   I – guess.
It was a long time ago now.

Jonah   How long?

Sam   Five years.

Jonah   And how long have I been gone?

Sam   Five years.

Jonah *nods.*

Beat.

Sam   It started late.
We were looking for you.

Jonah   I was on a train. Then a boat.

Sam   They made us start eventually, cos they had another one after us.

Pause.

Jonah   You need some women round here.
They've got answers to things we don't.
They're like Russians.

Sam   Women are like Russians?

Jonah   They know things . . .

A long silence.

I didn't want her to have it you know.

Sam   What?

Jonah   Nicola.
. . .
I tried to make her get rid of it.
. . .
. . .
She hated me anyway.
She was just fucking me to pass the time.
. . .
And she was into all kinds of stuff . . .
Do you see her at all?
She still live round here?

Sam   I – I think she moved away.

Jonah   Well.
It wasn't a good idea.
. . .
Had a proper sit down.
Said go take care of it.
But she wouldn't.
And I said,
I'd just pretend it didn't exist.
I said if she had it I wouldn't have anything to do with it.

Pause.

Sam   But you did.

Jonah   . . . yeah . . .

. . .

she was so small.
I never saw anything so small.

. . .

. . .

you know I only turned round.
She was right there in the, the – fucking –
Pushchair.
She just never sat still.
I just turned round for a *second* –

Sam   I know.

Jonah   And I told her about roads and cars,
and green men and red men.

. . .

I told her all of that stuff.

. . .

. . .

Stupid.

Pause.

Sam   It wasn't your –

Jonah   *Fucking Shut Up.*

Pause.

Everything's changed here.
I was in town –
All the pubs are closed up.
Lot of the shops.
The library . . .

. . .

Lot of boards on windows.
There's not much here any more.

. . .

Just a lot of spare time.

. . .

Pause.

Jonah   I think I came back to kill myself.

Pause.

Sam   You think . . .

Jonah   I don't know.

. . .

I haven't worked it out yet.

Beat.

Sam   I don't know what to do with that.

Jonah   Nothing.

Sam   Please don't.

Jonah   I'm not decided yet.

. . .

. . .

I'll let you know.

Pause.

I can see the moon.

. . .

That's still here at least.

Fade.

5.

The same.
We fade in during a show.
Laughter.
Jonah *sits on the bed, drinking.*

On the sofa is **Steve***, who has a snake.*

Sam   – and you feed him how many times a day?

Steve   You just got to give him a mouse, I can show you –
I haven't fed him . . .

He rummages in a box at his feet.

Sam   If you've just joined us, we're here with Steve, who
lives three doors down from me; and he's brought his pet
snake in to show us tonight.
That should tell you something about our struggle to book
guests.

Laughter.

Steve   So, he's already dead.

Sam   Oh it's a dead mouse.

Steve   You buy em frozen, like in packs –

Sam   *Packs* of dead mice?

Steve   Yeah.

Sam   Like fish fingers?

Laughter.

Steve   That way you don't have to keep a bunch of mice
alive.
Sometimes I get a live one cos people like to watch –

Sam   Well, people are disgusting.

Laughter.

Steve *dangles the mouse at the snake.*

Steve   When you first start feeding them the dead ones, you have to make like they're alive, like dangle them or whatever –

Sam   The thrill of the hunt.

Steve   Yeah, but Roger –

Sam   Roger's the snake's name, not the mouse.

Laughter.

Steve   The mouse doesn't have a name.

Sam   How depressing.

Laughter.

The snake isn't interested.

Sam   He's not looking hungry.

Steve   Nah, sometimes he's like this.
Sometimes he just doesn't want to eat or maybe he doesn't like the environment.

Sam   He's dissing my place?

Laughter.

Steve   He's just being a dick.

Sam   Well thanks for trying anyway, Steve.

Steve   That's cool –

Sam   Roger the snake everybody!

Applause.

Steve *puts the mouse away.*

Sam   So –

Jonah   How does it shit?

Beat.

Steve   I –

Jonah   How does it take a shit?

Steve   He kind of –

Sam   This is my uncle you can hear just off camera, ladies and gents.
He's a sophisticated man as you can tell.

Laughter.

Why don't you come up here and join us, Jonah?

Jonah *wanders on to the set and sits with* **Steve**.

Sam   This is my Uncle Jonah everybody, he's been staying with me the past few days.

Applause.

Jonah *waves to the 'audience'.*

Jonah   Good evening.

Sam   Jonah's desperate to know how your snake shits, Steve.

Laughter.

Jonah   How do they?

Sam   Enlighten us, please. Don't let us go through life ignorant.

Laughter.

Steve   It's just like other animals 'cept they only take a dump like every few days.

Sam   But they've got all the same . . . equipment.

Steve   Yeah –

Jonah   It's got an anus.

Steve   Wh –

Sam   I was trying to be a bit more delicate, but yes, that's basically what I was asking.

Laughter.

Steve   They've got an anus just at the end, where the scales are a bit weird.
It's got some special name I can't remember, but it's just like anything else, 'cept they only go every few days.

Sam   And what kind of . . . *consistency* are we talking here?

Groans.

Calm down, this is *science*!

Laughter.

Jonah   Is it like string?

Steve   No, it's just like normal. Sometimes it has bones in it from the mice.

Groans.

And once he got diarrhoea really bad and it was just like water everywhere, like he was swimming in it.

Groans.

Sam (*to* **Jonah**)   You see what happens when I let you on? You see what this has become now?

Laughter.

Jonah   I just think it's interesting. I'm interested in snakes.

Steve   Do you wanna hold him?

He passes the snake to **Jonah**.

Sam   Better you than me.

Steve   He's chill, he won't bite or anything.

Sam   Have you seen many snakes in your time, Jonah?

Jonah   I once –
I saw one in France.

Sam   You saw some snakes in France?

Jonah   I think it was France.

Sam   Do you get snakes in France?

Steve *shrugs.*

Jonah   It was a farm.
Someone's farm.
At night I was running in and stealing food –
They had grapes.
And tomatoes.
I stole a chicken once and crushed the head with a rock and
cooked it on a fire.

And I was in this wood, I was in the woods in the day, I'd hide
in the trees because this farmer, this French farmer, he knew
someone was stealing so he kept looking for me –
But I would climb up the trees and he wouldn't see me.

And once I was walking around the woods and I feel
something on my leg,
and there's this snake biting me –
It didn't slither away or anything, it just looked at me, it didn't
care.
Looked a bit like this one . . .

It didn't hurt much at first but then my ankle is swelling up big
like it's being pumped up with water.
It just keeps getting heavier and bigger; it's as thick as this, you
know?

And it hurts badly, it feels like it's filling up with acid –
So I just see red and pick up this fucking snake
and I grab his head and I grab his tail and I pull him till he's
two pieces.
Throw him on the ground and watch him curl up.
Then I get my knife –
I was carrying a knife back then for a lot of reasons –
And I just cut into my ankle –
Like a *balloon* –
To get the poison out.
Made a big hole in it so I could drain it –
Bleeding everywhere and there's all this pus and water –

And that helped but that thing was bad, I couldn't walk properly for weeks.

And that snake, I cooked him in those two pieces on my fire and ate him.
Tasted like plastic and ash.

Pause.

Sam   Okay, ah –

Steve   Give me my snake back, man –

Jonah *does.*

Sam   Steve, thanks for bringing Roger in, that's about all we have time for –

Jonah   We're stopping?

The music starts up.
Applause and cheering.

Sam   We'll be back tomorrow night, I look forward to seeing you then,
Good night!

He waves.
The music stops abruptly.

What's wrong with you?

Jonah   What?

Steve   You *murdered* a snake, man.

Jonah   He bit me.

Sam   Look –

Steve   Why did you let him hold my snake?

Sam   Steve, I'm sure –

Steve   He might've ripped it in half.

Jonah   Your snake didn't bite me.

Steve   Snakes bite, that's what they do, man.
You don't kill an animal for doing what they do.

Sam   You should get moving, Steve –

Steve *packs his snake away and heads out.*

Steve   What kind of man pulls snakes in half?

Jonah   It was only a snake.

Steve *clambers out of the window.*

Sam   Sorry about that, Steve –

Steve   Fuck you!

He's gone.

Beat.

Jonah   I didn't know he liked snakes so much.

Sam   You listened! You sat there and listened! He described himself as a fanatic!

Jonah   Well I didn't think he liked them *that* much.

Sam   You can't upset the guests, the show *is* the guests –

Jonah   Just get more guests –

Sam   I just structured a whole show around a guest whose only credential was that he owned a *snake*. I don't have a lot of choices –

Jonah   That snake deserved it.
I got a scar.

He lifts his trouser leg up. He has a big scar. One of many.

Sam   Jesus –

Jonah   How many people watched?

Sam   You look like a road map.

Jonah   How *many*?

Sam   I – (*Checks.*) Eight.

Jonah   Eight people? How many is usual?

Sam   Not as many as eight.

Jonah   I thought it was on the internet?

Sam   There's a lot of stuff on the internet –
Why were you living in France killing snakes?

Pause.

Jonah   I was just out there.
And I don't know it was France.
It might have been Spain.

Sam   What were you doing out there?
Why'd you leave us to go and do that?

Jonah *finds a beer and opens it.*

Jonah   I didn't leave you. I just left.

Beat.

Sam   Where did you go?

Jonah   I went lots of places.
I was in Wales for a while.
Greece.
All kinds of places.
I set off walking.

Sam   Why did you do that?

Pause.

Jonah (*shrugs*)   I just went away.

He lies down on the sofa and starts rolling a cigarette.

I'll have the sofa tonight.

Pause.

Sam   Is that it?

Jonah   What.

Sam   You don't think that requires a,
a,
an *explanation*, or –

Jonah   Why?

Sam   *Why*?
Can you not understand why I'm –
You don't tell me anything.

Jonah   Why do I need to?

Sam   Because you jumped in through my window after five
years of *nothing*.

Beat.

I didn't think I'd ever *see* you again.
I thought with all that happened you might've . . .
. . .
But apparently you were just roaming the world on some kind
of, of *vision* quest –

Jonah   I just went walking.

Sam   You *left*.
You ran away and I didn't have anyone to, to talk to about it.
About any of it.
. . .
Are you still on any –
. . .
Using . . .

Jonah   No.

Sam   I just –

Jonah   I told you. I came back.

Sam   That doesn't mean – You keep saying that! What does
that even *mean*?
Back from *where*? Where have you *been*?
. . .

And do you even have –
a,
a,
a,
plan –
Or do I have to just hide you in my room for ever now?

Jonah   You don't –

Sam   Why did you even *come* back?
Was it just so someone would *notice* if you killed yourself?

Pause.

I'm sorry – I mean –

Jonah   I'm just enjoying being here.
And I liked being on your show.

Beat.

We just need to work out how to get more people watching.
Maybe tomorrow we can –

Sam   Where did you get the money from?
That you're giving me?
. . .
The internet money –

Jonah   I stole it.

Sam   You *stole* it?

Jonah   Of course I stole it.
I don't even have my own clothes.

Sam   From where?

Jonah   Why would you want to know?

Sam   Where did you steal it from?

Jonah   A few places.
The newsagent.
I pickpocketed a / guy.

Sam   Oh my god –

Jonah   You said you needed money.

Sam   I didn't want you to *steal* it – It was only twenty quid for fuck's –

Jonah *pulls notes out of his crotch and flings them at* **Sam**.

Jonah   Well have some more then if that's not enough.

Sam   I don't *want* this.

Jonah   I'm trying to help you –

Sam   I don't need help –

Jonah   You're twenty-six and you're still living in a basement. Of course you need help.
All you've got is a worthless degree and a talk show no one watches.

Sam   It's not about that –

Jonah   I need to make sure you do something with at least one of those.
. . .
You're the only reason I ever tried at school or anything.
I watched you grow up.

Sam   And then you left me.

Jonah   I've come back.

Sam   To fuck everything up again!

The basement door flies open and **Bill** *hurtles downstairs in his pajamas.*

Bill   Will you shut the *fuck* up down here –
It's –

He spots **Jonah**.

A moment.

Jonah *stands up.*

Smiles.

Jonah   Hi Billy.

Pause.

Sam   Dad –

Bill   You're back, are you?

Jonah   Yeah.

Beat.

Bill *nods.*

Pause.

Jonah   I like your pajamas.

Bill *hurls himself at* **Jonah** *and they collapse, limbs flailing, on to the sofa, then the floor.*

They punch and tear at each other.

Sam   Whoawhoawhoastopitstopitdon't –

Jonah *is wiry and more experienced. He pins* **Bill** *down and smashes his head into the floor –*
But **Bill** *is the bigger of the two and propels* **Jonah** *off his back, and they fly off towards the stairs, grappling with each other.*

It's a vicious but scrappy fight.

Sam *mostly dithers and occasionally moves things out of their way.*

Sam   Stop it!

Bill *finally has* **Jonah** *pinned, a knee against his neck,* **Jonah**'s *palms squashing into his cheeks –*

Sam   Dad –

Jonah's *hands scrabble around the floor –*

Sam   Dad, he can't breathe –

Bill *pushes harder –*

Sam   *Dad!*

Jonah *brings a bottle smashing into* **Bill***'s head, who topples over.*
Jonah *scurries to a corner.*
They both catch their breath.

Sam   *Fuck –*

onah   I'm sorry . . .

Bill   You *glassed* me.

Sam   Are you alright?

Bill   I'm bleeding –

Jonah   I said sorry.

Sam   Is it bad? Does it hurt?

Bill   What is this? What's on me?

Sam   Oh –

Bill   It's wet – I'm wet –

Jonah   We piss in those bottles.

Bill   What?

Sam   That was a – A piss bottle Dad, sorry.

Jonah   We piss in those.

Beat.

Bill   This is your *piss.*

Jonah   It's a mix.

Ron (*from upstairs*)   What on earth's going on down there?

All   *Nothing.*

Blackout.

6.

The same.
Morning.
Sam, **Jonah**, **Bill** *and* **Ron** *stand, drinking mugs of tea.*

Sam *wears the suit jacket.*
Jonah *wears the shirt and tie.*
Bill *wears the suit trousers.*

A long silence.

Ron   So you'll be staying a while then, Jonah?

Jonah   Yeah –

Bill   Just until he gets his own place.

Pause.

Ron   Where will you sleep?

Jonah   / I'm fine on the sofa.

Sam   He sleeps here on the sofa, Grandad.

Ron   Just on here?

Jonah   Yeah.

Ron   Is it long enough for you?

Jonah   Yeah –

Ron   Do your feet not come off the end?

Jonah   It's fine.

Ron   Do you have enough bedding?

Bill   He's fine, Dad.

Pause.

They drink tea.

Ron   Are you thinking you'll stay in the area?

Jonah   I'll try.

Ron   Because you know we might be moving.

Jonah   / Yeah.

Bill   Not far.

Beat.

Ron   So you'll be looking for work then?

Jonah *nods.*

Ron   All three of you now, job hunting.

All nod.

Ron   Well, something'll come up.

Sam   Did you hear about the Kwik Booze job?

Bill   No.

Sam   You didn't get it?

Bill   I haven't heard.

Beat.

Jonah   Were you not qualified?

Beat.

Did you not have the qualifications to work in a cage?

Bill   You don't need a degree in Russian books to work –

Sam   / Stop –

Ron   Don't bicker, boys.

Beat.

Jonah   *Literature.*

Beat.

Ron   Is there sugar in this Sam?

Sam   Uh –
I'll get some.

He tromps off upstairs.

A long pause.

Jonah *pulls at his tie.*

A long pause.

Sam *reappears with* **Ron**'s *tea.*

Ron   Thank you.

Jonah   Have you got any biscuits?

Bill   You want biscuits, you –

Sam   We've not got any biscuits.

Ron   Are you hungry, Jonah?

Jonah   I'm alright –

Ron   It's about time for lunch, would you say?

Bill   I don't know if we've got –

Ron   There's a bit of ham in the fridge isn't there?

Jonah   / I'm fine.

Sam   And cheese.

Ron   That's right, we've some cheese in there too.

Bill   Not much.

Ron   Shall we head upstairs for some food then?

Jonah   / I'm okay really –

Bill   We don't have all day, Dad.

Ron   We've plenty of time, come on –

He heads upstairs.

See what we can find, eh?

They all follow.

Ron   Sure we've got some oatcakes lying around somewhere as well –

Bill   We finished those.

Jonah *hasn't moved.*
Sam *stops on the stairs.*

Sam   What?

Jonah   What.

Sam   Are you coming up?

Jonah   Yes.

Beat.

Sam   Are you alright?

Jonah   I'm coming.
. . .
I'm fine.

Beat.

Sam   Sorry about the –
Arguing.
Before.

Jonah   Right.

Sam   And –
Dad –
Sorry he's being a dick –

Jonah   Don't say that.

Sam   What?

Jonah   Don't say that about him.

Beat.

Right?

Sam   Okay – Sorry.

Pause.

Sam   Do you still –

Jonah   Who's on the show tonight?

Sam   The – Oh, no one.

Jonah   No one.

Sam   I can't – I didn't have time to – I probably won't do it tonight.

Jonah   You're not gonna do it.

Sam   I don't really – With everything that's –

Jonah   You have to do it.

Sam   I –

Jonah   It's important.

Sam   It's, it's not really.

Jonah   Is it because I'm here?

Sam   No –

Jonah   I'll leave.

Sam   No, it's –

Jonah   If you stop, I'll leave.

Sam   Don't.
. . .
It's not that –
I'll do it tomorrow.
Tomorrow night, I'll do it.

Beat.

Jonah   It's important.

Sam   Okay.

Jonah   You have to do it.

Sam   I, I will.

. . .

I will.

. . .

. . . what you said the other night –
Are you still feeling –

Jonah   Forget about that.

Sam   Do you want to maybe, *talk* to someone? We could
call, uh, Samaritans or –

Jonah   Forget it. I'm fine.

Beat.

Sam   What about the, the stealing, are you –

Ron (*from off*)   Are you coming boys?

Beat.

Jonah   Don't worry about it.
Do your show.

Beat.

Sam   You –

Jonah   Can you stop *fussing* me?

. . .

I'll be up in a minute.

Sam *heads upstairs.*

Pause.

Jonah *pulls at his tie.*

He finds a can of lager and opens it.

Takes a swig.

Untucks his shirt.

Looks at the ceiling.

He wipes his forehead.

He turns on the baby monitor.

Ron   – tin of corned beef in the cupboard there, Sam.

Bill   Let's not go mad.

Sam   We have to eat Dad. You can't ration us.

Bill (*unintelligible*).

Sam   I know –

Ron (*unintelligible*).

Sam   It'll be in the side cupboard, Grandad.
. . .
Not that one, the other –
Yeah.

Pause.

Jonah *pulls at his tie, tightens it until he turns red, splutters, then lets go.*

Ron   Well it's nice to have you all under one roof again.

Bill (*unintelligible*).

Sam   He's – He's gone to the toilet or something –

Bill (*unintelligible*).

Sam   We're not using the bottles any more.

Ron   Will this be enough do you think?

Bill   It's fine, Dad.

Jonah *heads upstairs.*

Ron   And we've a little bit of – There you are, we've laid on a bit of a spread here, Jonah.

Bill   Not much of a spread.

Jonah   It's fine.

Ron   Dig in, dig in boys.

Pause.

Ron   Have you got yourself –

Bill   He's fine Dad, don't fuss.

Ron   Well I'm just –

Jonah   I'm alright.

Pause.

Ron   There's a bit more of that if you want it.

Bill   We don't have to eat it all just because it's in front of us.

Sam   Stop being so tight Dad.

Pause.

Bill   Excuse me.

Pause.

He comes downstairs.

Looks around.

He starts searching the room –

*He looks under **Sam**'s mattress, then under the bed –*

He looks through the books, checking the spines of any hardbacks –

He sticks his hands down the back of the sofa –

It's fast and not very thorough.

*He finds **Jonah**'s abandoned beer and drinks.*

Pause.

He starts padding the pillows down –

Ron   Are you glad to be back then, Jonah?

Bill *freezes –*

Jonah   Yeah.

Bill *realises it's the baby monitor.*

Ron   Have you – Does Liz know you're back?

Jonah   No –

Ron   Oh well, you should give her a call –

Sam   He didn't know she'd moved, Grandad.

Ron   Oh, yes. Well, you know –
She's very close.
See her every day, don't we Sam?

Sam   Pretty much.

Ron   We're all still friendly with one another.
We're all still together.
She's a new husband now, called Pete.
. . .
You should let her know you're back.
. . .
Has Sam told you about his show that he does?

Jonah   Yes.

Ron   It's on the internet, you know.

Sam   It's nothing.

Jonah   It's not nothing.

Ron   No, it's very impressive. Does it all himself, you know.
You should have Jonah on, I bet you've got some stories, don't you?
Have you been travelling all over the place?

Beat.

Jonah   Yeah.
A lot of –
. . .
I've come back now.

Bill *puts the pillows back.*

Jonah   It's good to be home.

Fade.

7.

The same.
Night.
It's raining a little.
Sam *and* **Bill** *stand considering each other.*
Sam *is shirtless.*
Bill *has two beers.*

Bill   Put a shirt on . . .

Sam   I just finished the show, I'm getting dressed –

He takes his trousers off.

Bill   Well I want to talk to you, can you put some clothes on?

Sam   Why can't you talk to me like this?

Bill   It's . . . slovenly.
. . .
Put a top on.

Beat.

Sam *fishes a T-shirt from a pile and puts it on.*
Bill *flings him a beer.*

Bill   Take a bit of pride in your appearance.
That's all the working man's got.

They open their beers.

Sam   We're not working men.

Bill   You know what I mean.

Pause.

How was your show?

Sam   You don't care.

Bill   I'm asking you.

Sam   Why are you up so late?

Bill   I don't have anything to get up for tomorrow.

Pause.

Sam   I had this guy who used to be in a band who were on last week.

Bill   He's not in the band any more?

Sam   Ed Heslop . . .

Bill   Neil's son?

Sam   Yeah. Well.
He was in a band – 'Misguided Fury' – who were on last week.
They woke you up I think.
But they've split now.
So now he sings angry acoustic songs about how much he hates them.

Bill   Misguided . . .

Sam   Misguided Fury.

Bill   Were they good?

Sam   No they were fucking awful.
They could have done with some guidance.

Bill   Did you say that on the show?

Sam   Yeah.

Bill   Did people laugh?

Sam   People always laugh Dad, it's a laugh track.

Beat.

Bill   Who was on yesterday?

Sam   No one, I didn't do it yesterday.

Bill   You didn't do it?

Sam   Why do you care? You always say it's a waste of time.

Bill   Why didn't you do it?

Sam   Because, just – I just didn't.
Sometimes I might not.
It doesn't matter.
. . .
Anyway.
I don't know why I'm telling you.

Pause.

Bill   Jonah out?

Sam *nods.*

Bill   How long has he been here?

Beat.

Sam   Few days.

Bill   He told you to hide him?

Sam *nods.*

Pause.

Bill   What I said –
The other night . . .

Sam   You don't need to be sorry.

Bill   Well –

Sam   You meant it.

Bill   I didn't –
Not . . .
I was a bit over the top –

Sam   You said it's his fault Grandma died.

Bill   I – Don't say that.

Sam   That's what you said.

Bill   . . . he didn't help things.

Sam   He lost his *daughter*.

Beat.

Bill   We all know that.

Pause.

He pings his ring pull.

We don't need to get into all this.

Sam   Course not, we don't talk about anything in this family.

Bill   I don't think talking would . . .
. . .
anyway.

Beat.

Is he smoking anything?

Sam   *No.*

Bill   Right.

Sam   If you weren't expecting him to –

Bill   I'm not expecting anything –

Sam   Course you are.

Bill   I'm *asking*.

Beat.

I'm asking.

Beat.

You know he was always –
Long before all of what –
. . .
You know he didn't go to his graduation?

Beat.

Sam   What does that have to do with anything?

Bill   He was the first in the family to get a degree, and he wouldn't do the,
the ceremony.
With the robes and all that.

Beat.

Sam   So?

Bill   So he didn't tell anyone he wasn't going.
We all turned up in our Sunday best,
Me and your grandma and grandad.
Big proud moment.
You know what she was like, crying before we've even got there.
Sit down. Your grandad's chatting to anyone who'll listen.
And we're sitting watching everyone else walk up and get
their, ah, scroll –
And we get to S.
And he wasn't there.

. . .

Waited for him all day.
Went to the drinks afterwards and everything.
Stood around in our smart clothes.

. . .

Your grandma couldn't –

Sam   Maybe he –

Bill   Turned up a few days later, fumes heaving off him,
back to borrow money.
They gave him it of course.

. . .

I don't know how he managed to even pass.

. . .

. . .

And,
Obviously,
She didn't make it to yours.

Pause.

He drinks.

Sam   You never told me that.

Bill   Why would I?

Sam   But you don't tell me anything –

Bill   What use would it have been to you?

Beat.

He was your hero.
No use . . .

. . .

Pause.

Anyway.
You'll tell me if he –
If something goes wrong.

Pause.

Sam.

Sam   You only talk about anything if you've got something
bad to say.

Bill   That's not –

Sam   So negative. All the time. Can't you just ever talk to
me normally?
About anything?

Pause.

Bill   He's not your responsibility.
You'll tell me.
If something –

Sam   Yes.

Bill   I won't gloat.
I just need to know.
Alright?

Sam   Alright, Dad.

Jonah*'s forehead thumps on the window.*

Bill   Here's trouble.

He goes to leave.
Jonah *opens the window and slips in, carrying a record player.*

Jonah   Look what I got.

He shakes the rain out of his hair.

Bill   Where'd you / find that?

Sam   What is it?

Jonah   Turntable.

Bill   Where'd you take that from.

Jonah   I found it in the street.

Bill   You just *found* it –

Jonah   Yes I found it. In the street. I said.
You sold the old one, I thought Sammy might like it.

He wrestles with **Sam**.

Bill   I sold the old one to pay the electric bill.

Jonah   Yeah, you're a hero.

Bill   I never –
I never even *tried* to sell any of your –
Your computer, *two* cameras –

Sam   I know Dad.

Bill   I'm not the –

Sam   It's fine.

Jonah *plugs in the record player.*

Bill   Running round in the rain, in your T-shirt.
Did you go down the job centre?

Jonah   Why are you up so late?

Bill   Did you go to the job centre?

Jonah   No one gets work at the job centre Billy, everyone knows that.

Bill   So you didn't go.

Jonah   I went round asking in shops.

Bill   Dressed like that.

Jonah   You don't need to wear a suit to stack shelves. You'd know that, wouldn't you?

He squares up against **Bill***, mocking.*

Jonah   You're up past your bedtime.

Bill   Give over.

Sam   Don't argue.
Always arguing, it's boring.

Pause.

Jonah *takes* **Bill***'s beer.*

Bill   I'll see you in the morning.

Jonah   Did you do your show?

Sam   Yes.

Jonah   Did you hear he stopped?

Sam   I didn't / stop –

Jonah   It's important. You have to tell him to do it.

Bill   / I –

Jonah   I bet you don't even understand it.

Sam   I did it. I'm doing it.
I don't know why you care so much. No one watches anyway.

Jonah   Give me a record.

Bill   The records are gone.

Jonah   He has one left.

Sam   I don't think we need to –

Jonah   Give it.

Sam *reluctantly gets the record he kept.*

Bill   It won't just –

Jonah   It's got a speaker in it.

Bill   Well just keep it down.
It's late.

Jonah   Aren't you staying for a dance?

Bill   Probably doesn't even work.

The needle hits the record.
Dottie West's 'Is This Me' pipes out of the tiny built-in speaker.

Jonah   Such a pessimist.

He waltzes around the room with a reluctant **Sam** –

Jonah   You'll never –
Enjoy life –
Billy Starling –

Sam *wriggles free.*

Jonah   Not with that attitude.
. . .
What is this?

Sam   . . . Dottie West.

Pause.

Jonah   *This* is what you like?

Sam   / It's Grandma's.

Bill   It's Mum's.

. . .

It was one of Mum's records.

Pause.

Jonah   Oh.

They listen.

After a while, **Ron**'s *legs appear at the top of the stairs, unnoticed.*

The song plays for quite a while.

Jonah *seems confused.*

Eventually **Ron** *heads back upstairs.*

Jonah *stops the record –*

Jonah   I don't remember this –

He breaks the record over his knee.

Sam *winces.*

Bill   What did you do that for?

Pause.

Jonah *looks at the pieces.*

Bill   You have to break everything.

Jonah   I'm sorry Sam.

Sam   . . . it's alright.

Jonah   I just didn't –

He tries to press it back together –

Maybe if we get some –

Bill   It's broken. That's it.
Well done.

Pause.

Jonah   Sorry.

He picks up the sleeve to put the pieces back in –

I didn't mean to –

A small photo flutters out of the sleeve.

Beat.

He picks it up.

Sam   Hey, don't –

Jonah *recoils and drops the photo.*

Pause.

Bill   It's / alright –

Jonah   Why do you have that?

Sam   I don't – / I just –

Bill   It's just a photo –

Jonah *grabs* **Sam** *and hurls him across the room.*

Bill   Hey!

Jonah   *You don't do that*!

Pause.

Bill   Jonah.

Jonah   He has a picture of her –

Bill   Don't touch him again.

Jonah   He shouldn't –

Bill   Don't touch him.

Sam   I just kept it –
I was scared of forgetting . . .
I'm sorry . . .

Bill   There's nothing wrong with that.
. . .
Is there.

Jonah.

. . .

Do you want to wake Dad up?

Pause.

Jonah *squirms.*

Jonah   I didn't remember she looked like that.

Bill   Sit down.

Beat.

Just calm down, we're alright.

Beat.

Jonah   I'm holding her . . .

Bill   Just sit down, and we'll –

Jonah *bolts across the room –*

Bill   Jonah –

– and out the window.

Pause.

Sam   We need to go after him –

Bill   Leave him be.

Sam   Dad –

Bill   He just needs a minute.

Sam   *Dad*, he told me –
He – He told me he might kill himself.

Beat.

Bill   I doubt –

Sam   We have to go *find* him.

Beat.

Sam   *Dad* –

Bill   Alright.
Stay here.

Sam   We should both –

Bill   You stay here.
Case he comes back.
Okay?

Sam *nods.*

Bill   He'll be alright –

Sam   Don't say anything to him –

Bill   I won't –

Sam   Don't shout at him.
You always –
Don't have a go at him.

Beat.

Bill   Okay.

Beat.

Sam   I didn't mean to –
I didn't think he'd see it –

Bill   It's not your fault.
. . .

He picks up the broken record.

Bill   Must've looked like a ghost.

Blackout.

8.

The same.
The next day.
Early evening.
Ron *stands.*

Sam *looks out the window.*

Pause.

Ron   Shall we get started on tea, Sam?

Sam   In a – I think –

. . .

Beat.

Ron   Has he been gone a while?

Sam   Since last night.

Ron   And you're worried about him?

Sam   Course I am . . .
Of course I am.

Pause.

Ron   I'm sure he's fine.

Sam   I don't think he *is* fine –
I don't think he is . . .

He heads out.

I should go and look, / if we're both looking then –

Ron   Sam. *Sam.*
If he doesn't want to be found, he won't be.

Beat.

Alright?
He's not for you to worry about.

Pause.

Sam   Are you still angry with him?

Ron   *Angry* with him?

Sam   Not – I mean –

Ron   Why would I be *angry* with him?

Pause.

Sam   You don't ever feel angry.

Ron   Sometimes, of course you do.

Sam   You do.

Ron   About some things.
I feel angry with the bank.
I feel angry with this town.
I couldn't feel angry with Jonah.
What would I have to be angry about?

Sam   . . . Because of Grandma.

Ron   Your grandma was never angry at Jonah.

Sam   But he –
All of the, the drugs.
And the – He stole so much money from her. And you.
And the fighting and the violence and –

Ron   It was what it was. He went through a lot.

Sam   Even before that, though. Even before that he was –

Ron   You can't tell anyone how to live.
. . .
Specially not Jonah.
All you can do is be around if things go wrong.

Pause.

Sam   I wish we talked about it more.
. . .
We never talked about it.

Beat.

Ron   What would you –

Upstairs, the front door slams.

Sam   Hello?

Bill *thumps down the stairs.*

Bill   Is he here?

Sam   No –

Bill   Has he been here?

Sam   No –

Ron   / He's not been back.

Bill   Don't fuck me around / Sam.

Ron   Hey now –

Sam   He's not *here*.

Beat.

What is it?

Bill   He's been breaking into places, he's been helping himself to the tills –

Sam   I know . . .

Bill   You *know*?

Sam   He, he said – I couldn't stop him –

Bill   What did I *tell* you? / What did I *say* about telling me everything?

Ron   / William.

Sam   How could I tell you?

Bill   Are you a *moron*? That's, assisting a criminal or some sort of –

Ron   *William.*
Does no good shouting about anything.

Bill   Dad, he's setting fire to half the town.

Sam   What?

Beat.

Bill   The off-licence, and –

Sam   He's set *fire* to –

Bill   Can you not *hear* me?

Ron *heads upstairs, unnoticed.*

Sam   Stop shouting, I don't – What do you mean he's –

Bill   There are buildings on fire.

Sam   Where?

Bill   Here. This town.
There are *fires*.

The window smashes.
Jonah, *barefoot and shirtless, pushes his way through the glass, adding to a number of cuts on his torso and rips to his trousers.*
He carries records and bottles of spirits and is slightly blackened and sooty.
He stinks of smoke.

Jonah   I don't know why I don't just use the front door.

Bill   What have you done?

Sam   / Jonah –

Jonah   I've done all sorts. I've been busy –

He drops the records.

Went and got your records back Sam,

He fishes bundles of notes out of his trousers and hurls them at **Bill**.

Jonah   And that's your mortgage payments for a while, you can keep the house now, eh?

Bill   Sit down.

Jonah   Why?

Bill   Sit *down*.

Jonah   *No*.
. . .
Is that not enough?
Here –

More money.

Jonah   And help yourself, I haven't felt like drinking anyway –

He chucks the bottles. One smashes on the floor.

Sam   / Please –

Jonah *takes his tobacco pouch out of his crotch and rolls a cigarette.*

Jonah   I burnt that place to the ground.
I went there, to that off-licence –
That place –
They wouldn't even give you a chance, so I went there and
burned the fucking place down.

Bill   That's not what I wanted –

Jonah   It's what *I* wanted.
. . .
I went in,
some guy's there,
like Sam, Sam's age,
and I just tell him, I've got this petrol, I'm not aiming to hurt
you, press your alarm, whatever you need to do, but get out
that cage and out the door because I'm going to burn this all
down.
I didn't hurt him –
I didn't want to hurt anyone,
I just said you'd best head out because this place is going off.
And I did it and it went up angry.
All kinds of flames and fury.
Then I went and torched that lumber yard that sacked you.

That was harder though cos there wasn't any fucking lumber in it.

He lights his cigarette.

Bill   They didn't sack me. They shut down.
Places shut down –

Jonah   *Fuck* them.
They've got a responsibility to you, to everyone working there.
Keep it open, make it work. He just wants to pay off his third car or –

Bill   It's not like that.

Jonah   *Course it's like that!*
It's always like that.
I've been around.
I've seen half the world. They're all like that.
. . .
. . .
You're calm.
Considering.

Bill   I just want us to work this out.

Jonah   And you're near silent.

Sam   I don't –

Jonah   I've got your internet bills paid there for months.
You should be grateful.

Sam   I – I am –

Bill   Don't humour him.

Jonah   Don't tell him –
You're always telling him what he can't do.
Let him make his own mind up.
You don't have the answers.
You can't even provide for him.
Deadbeat fucking –

Bill   He's twenty-six, Jonah.
I shouldn't have to provide for him.

Pause.

Jonah   I thought we could go and do the job centre next.
We could go do it together as a family.

Bill   No.

Jonah   And then that supermarket that used you for slave labour –

Bill   No.

Jonah   What about it Sam?
Something we can bond over.
. . .
Why should we be at the bottom of everything?

Pause.

Bill   You're done for tonight.

Jonah   I could flatten you.

Bill   Okay.

Jonah   I could tear you to pieces.
I could rip you in half.
You're an old man and you can't even stop me.
You're my big brother and I could just break you –

Bill   I don't want to fight you any more.

Jonah   Cos you're *weak* –

Bill   I'm just tired.

Pause.

Jonah   I'm just standing up for you.
I'm doing all the things you should've –
Pride is all men like us *have* –

Bill   What do you want.

Beat.

Bill   What do you *want*.

Jonah   I told you, I –

Bill   What's your plan? What's next?
Are you going to kill yourself or have you changed your mind about that?
. . .
Maybe you're thinking you'll just leave again.
Maybe you can just run away –

Jonah   I'm not running away.

Bill   Well whatever it is you do. Whatever it is you do when you disappear.

Jonah   You want me out the way.

Bill   I just want you to find what it is you want.

Jonah   What did you ever want? You never wanted *anything*.

Bill   I wanted my family.

Jonah   And you couldn't even make Liz stay –

Bill   I can't make anyone do anything.

Jonah   Because you're a loser.
You couldn't stop them taking Dad's house –

Bill   It was too late for anyone to stop that.

Jonah   You can't even get a job.

Bill   I will eventually.

Pause.

Jonah *quivers and shakes.*

Jonah   I was always her favourite.

Bill   Okay.

Jonah   She loved me most.

Bill   I know.

Beat.

Jonah   And I . . .

. . .

Bill   You hated her.
Because she couldn't fix everything.

Beat.

Jonah *looks at the window.*

He looks at **Sam**.

Jonah   This is such shit . . .

. . .
You're a pair of fucking . . .
I'm not even –
I've done everything I thought –

. . .

Beat.

I went to *Russia*.

. . .
. . .
I went to places I can't pronounce and places I'd never heard of.

And sometimes I had no shoes and sometimes I ate out of bins –
and I would fight people in alleys and broken buildings and I walked till my feet were chapped with blood.
And I was alone.

. . .
I didn't open my mouth for weeks.
I didn't speak.
I lived on a boat in the middle of an ocean.
I slept in storm drains and in burnt-out cars.
I slept on a pile of dead dogs

. . .
I walked so far.

I walked so far to make sense of everything and, and forget –

. . .

It didn't work.

. . .

And then I came back and that hasn't worked either.

Pause.

I just wish she'd never had it . . .

Bill   No you don't.

Jonah   I wasn't meant to be someone's Dad . . .

Bill   It was an accident.

Jonah   Shut the *FUCK UP*.

Beat.

Stop talking. Why are you *talking* so much?

Pause.

Ron *appears on the stairs during the following, unnoticed.*

Jonah   Hit me.

Bill   No.

Jonah   Fucking cunt –

Bill   Sit down.

Jonah   Everything I've done and you don't even want to –

Bill   Sit down on the *sofa*, Jonah.

Jonah (*approaching* **Sam**)   What about you then –

Bill   Jonah.

Jonah   Come on, let's fucking go –

Bill   Sit *down* Jonah!

Jonah   I won't *ever* sit down!

Ron   Jonah.

Jonah *whirls around and looks at* **Ron** *on the stairs.*

Jonah   What? What do you want?

Ron   Why don't you sit down on the sofa there.

Bill   / Dad –

Jonah   Stay out of this –

Ron   I'll sit with you, how about that.

He goes and sits down on the sofa.

Here. Come and sit next to me here.

Jonah   Why.

Ron   Because I'm asking you to.

Pause.

Jonah *looks around, wary.*

Pause.

He sits next to **Ron***, as far away as he can.*

Ron   Now. I'm going to show you something, alright?

He gets his wallet out of his pocket.

He opens it and shows **Jonah***, who springs up and away.*

Bill   Dad –

Ron   Come on, sit down. It's alright.

Jonah *shakes his head.*

Ron   Sit down Jonah.

Beat.

Jonah *sits.*

Ron   Now look again.

Jonah *looks.*

Ron   You recognise all of these don't you.
Who's that.

Pause.

Jonah   Mum.

Ron   That's right. And there's you and your brother, of course.
Do you recognise this happy chap here?

Jonah *shakes head.*

Ron   That's Sam, when he was a baby.
Do you remember when he was born?

Jonah *shakes head.*

Ron   It was a very sunny day. I remember.
We all went in the car. Your brother drove us.
Me and your mum and you.
We picked you up from school and went straight there.
To the hospital.
And we went in, and there's Liz, sat up in bed,
And Sam's there.
She's holding him.
Brand new. Bout this big.
His face was all scrunched up, like he was angry to be out.
But there he was.
Grandson. Nephew.
Do you remember that?
You were about seven. You wouldn't let anyone else hold him.

He smiles.

And who's this here?

Jonah *shakes head.*

Ron   Come on, who's this.

Beat.

Jonah   . . .

Ron   Hm?

Jonah   Ellie.

Beat.

Ron   I bet you've not said her name for a very long time.

Pause.

I know you miss her.
We all do.
And we all miss your mother.
But it's alright to talk about them.
It'd be a mistake to try and forget them.
It's a terrible thing to forget.

And it was a terrible, cruel accident to happen that took your
Ellie from us.
And I know it'll always hurt.
But I'm so glad we got to meet her.
. . .
We're all so lucky to have each other.
Don't you think?

He smiles.

Beat.

The doorbell rings.

Ron   Can you go and get that William, that'll be the police
just now.

Sam   Wait – police –

Bill   You called the police –

Ron   Go on.

Beat.

Bill *heads upstairs.*

Sam   Grandad –

Ron *stands* **Jonah** *up.*

Ron   Now, you can take these with you, alright?

He takes the photos out of his wallet and gives them to **Jonah**, *who doesn't take his eyes off them.*

Sam   Wait – Grandad –

Ron   And we'll come see you first chance we get, alright?

Sam   No, we can't –

Ron   Jonah needs to go and talk to the police, Sam.

Sam   But –

Ron   There's no use pretending otherwise.

Bill *comes downstairs.*

Sam   We *can't* –

Jonah   It's alright.

Beat.

Sam   No, it's not –
You need –
You can't just –
This isn't right –

Jonah   I, ah –
. . .
I reckon it might do me some good.
. . .
Bit of structure.
Routine.
. . .
Get some reading done . . .

Pause.

Sam   But –
. . .

Jonah   It's okay.

Ron   Put a shirt on Jonah, tidy yourself up a bit.

Jonah *picks up the Lincoln shirt from the floor and pulls it on.*

Sam   Wait –

Jonah   I gave your Moby-Dick to a kid in the park, sorry.

Sam   I don't care, that's –

Jonah   I told him what it was and he was interested in whales so I gave him it.
I'll get you another.

Beat.

I'd best go.

Sam   Just go out the window, just run off –

Jonah   I'm –
I'm tired.
. . .
I'm really tired.

Sam   Dad, don't let him go.

Jonah   It's okay.
Don't waste your time worrying about me –

Sam *hugs him.*

Pause.

Jonah *pats his back.*

Jonah   I'll ah –
I'll be alright.

He unwraps **Sam***'s arms and pats him on the shoulder.*

He goes over to **Bill***.*

They stand there.

Bill *rubs the back of his neck.*

Bill   Well . . .

Jonah (*nods*)

. . .

He claps him on the arm.

Sorry.

Bill *nods.*

Jonah *heads up the stairs.*

Ron   Mind how you go, Jonah.

Jonah   Yeah.

He looks around. Looks at his photos.

. . . I'll see ya.

He leaves.

We listen to the footsteps and voices upstairs.

Pause.

We hear the front door shut.

Pause.

Sam   I –

. . .

What time is it?

Bill   Sam –

Sam   Because I have –
It's time, I've got to –

Sam *starts picking up/turning on his cameras and booting up his computer.*

Sam   I can't be late, I have to get on, I've got to –

Bill   Just calm down for a minute.

Sam   No, I can't, I've got to –

He pulls a tie on over his T-shirt.

Sam   I've got to be consistent –

Bill   I don't think you're in a fit state to –

Sam   *I can't give up*!

Beat.

Bill   It's not giving up –

Sam   You don't *get* it. You *never* have.

Ron   Sam –

Sam   I'm on *every* night, Monday through Friday.
That's the point.
That's the *point* of it.
Something people can *rely* on.
I'll always be there. Whatever happens, I will *be* there.
Because people need a sense of order and they need
ah,
ah,
ah,
comfort.
And who knows, who knows maybe I'll end up with some kind
of bigger,
ah,
audience,
and then maybe,
I don't know,
I know I'm not any good but I'm trying and there's something
to be said for that
and maybe someone will see it and pick us up and then I can
start bringing in some money,
and then maybe we can stay here or even move to a bigger
house where my dad doesn't have to sleep on a mattress on the
floor in his *living* room,
and maybe we can afford to have a bit of variety in our diets,
and maybe we could just *live* a little better because it seems like
this is the only thing I have at the moment. No one else seems
to want me.

No one wants to employ me,
I don't blame them,
I don't have any skills and I don't have any experience, and a
third-class degree in American literature isn't much to anyone
so I might as well just keep plugging away at this and hope
something comes out of it.
. . .
I can *try*.

I'm allowed to try.

Beat.

He goes and sits behind the desk.

Bill   Don't –
Maybe let's talk about it –

Sam *(to cameras)*   Good evening, welcome to The Sam
Starling Show, I'm sorry we're a little bit late, and I'm sorry
I've dispensed with the music, and the,
the monologue, but I thought we'd get right into it –
. . .
. . .
I don't –
. . .
We've not got anyone specific, ah –
. . .
booked for tonight, but –
. . .
. . .

Pause.

Ron   Sam.

Sam *looks over at his dad and grandad.*

Pause.

Please welcome to the show, Ron and Bill Starling!

Music, applause.

Sam *stands, applauding, waving them over.*

They don't move.

He loops the music and applause over again, waves more.

Ron *makes his way over and sits down.*

Sam *loops the applause again.*

Bill *stands there, awkward.*

The applause loops again.

Pause.

Bill *makes his way over and sits down next to* **Ron***.*

Sam   Thank you. For, ah, joining us tonight –
And thanks for making us wait, you know how to work a crowd.

Laughter.

Ron *smiles at the audience.*

Ron   Thank you.

Sam   Uh, no, thank you.

Bill   Sam, this isn't –
Is anyone watching this?

Sam   We can only hope, Dad.
I'm sure you're all aware by now that this is my dad and grandad. Don't they look fantastic tonight, ladies and gents?

Applause.

Sam   Beautiful. We're very lucky to have you here with us –

Ron   Do I talk at the camera, Sam?

Bill   You're supposed to talk to him, Dad.

Ron   I just talk to you?

Sam   Talk to me like you just met me, Grandad.

Ron   Okay. Hello.

Laughter.

Sam   Hi Grandad. I'm sure you can all tell, we're going to have a great show.

Laughter.

He turns to **Bill** *and* **Ron**.

Sam   So.

Blackout.

Notes

The Show

Sam has a small remote hooked up to his laptop that controls the music, canned laughter, applause and other audience noises.

He has about three to four different laugh tracks which he uses depending on the level of laugh needed.

Sam has modelled the show on classic American late-night talk shows: The Tonight Show with Johnny Carson and Late Night with David Letterman.

Drink

A lot of beer is drunk throughout the play; despite this, no one should ever seem even remotely drunk.

Interval

If an interval is required it would fall best between 5 and 6.

Pomona

Pomona was commissioned and first performed on 1 April 2014 by the Royal Welsh College of Music and Drama with the following cast and creative team:

Harry	Ella Cook
Keaton	Annes Elwy
Larry	Claire Inie-Richards
Moe	Sam Rix
Ollie	Thalissa Teixeira
Charlie	Bertie Taylor-Smith
Zeppo	Joe Windsor

Director   Ned Bennett
Set Designer   Isa Shaw-Abulafia
Costume Designer   Helen Rodgers
Lighting Designer   Sam Griesser
Sound Designer   Neil Campbell
Musical Composition   Ray Leung, Hugh Sheehan, Julian Williamson
Fight Director   Kev McCurdy
Assistant Production Manager   Cam Balfour
Stage Manager   Hannah Royall
Deputy Stage Manager   Adam Elbir
Assistant Stage Manager   Kate Louisa Ashford
Richard Burton Theatre Chief Technician   Nicholas Cummings
Richard Burton Theatre Technician   Megan Hastings
Production Manager   Daz James
Stage Management Supervisor   Claire Porter
Technical Supervisor   Jon Turtle

Pomona was subsequently produced at the Orange Tree Theatre, London, on 12 November 2014 with the following cast and creative team:

Zeppo	Guy Rhys
Ollie	Nadia Clifford
Fay	Rebecca Humphries
Keaton	Sarah Middlcton
Gale	Grace Thurgood/Rochenda Sandall*
Moe	Sean Rigby
Charlie	Sam Swann

*Rochnda Sandall took over the part of Gale for the play's transfer to the National Theatre

Director   Ned Bennett
Designer   Georgia Lowe
Lighting Designer   Elliot Griggs
Composer and Sound Designer   Giles Thomas
Movement Director   Polly Bennett
Fight Director   Pam Donald
Assistant Designer   Katy Mills
Casting Consultant   Juliet Horsley
Production Manager   Stuart Burgess
Deputy Stage Manager   Becky Flisher
Assistant Stage   Sophie Acreman
Managers   Rachel Middlemore

Active Ingredients

Seven actors to perform the following roles:

Ollie, *female*
Fay, *female*
Gale, *female*
Keaton, *female, small*

Zeppo, *male*
Charlie, *male*
Moe, *male*

Recommended Consumption

In Scenes Seven and Seventeen, the lines are split between the actors as the director sees fit, with the exception of those marked.

The actors enter the space with the audience, and remain on stage throughout.

Minimal set and props.

There are no entrances or exits unless stated. They just

Are.

Notes

A question without a question mark denotes a flatness of tone.
A dash (−) indicates an interruption of speech or train of thought.
An ellipsis (. . .) indicates either a trailing off, a breather, a shift, or a transition.
A slash (/) indicates where the next line of dialogue interrupts or overlaps.

/ one.

3:24 a.m.

The M60 ring road.

A car circles the city.

Zeppo *drives.*

Ollie *listens.*

A **Figure** *in a Cthulhu mask sits in the back.*

Zeppo *eats Chicken McNuggets and talks at a ferocious pace.*

Zeppo   – nazis take em to this cave, like a basin or something, a basin in the rock, and they have the ark sat there all gold and shiny, and they're all sat in these folding chairs – I don't know where they got them from, they must just travel with them – And they have this priest guy to open it, and the sweaty dude with the coat hanger, he's there, and Belloq's there,
And Indy and Marion are like, tied to this pole at the back –
And then the priest opens the ark, and this dust sprays out, and it's all mysterious,
and the nazis are all leaning in trying to see what's going on –
But it's just *sand*, like it's just *sand* in there. And they look *gutted*. Like, can't believe how many people died for this and it's just *sand* – we've been carrying this fucking box the whole way and it was just *sand*? We could've dumped this out miles back.
So the coat-hanger guy just starts laughing, and the nazis are looking at Belloq like 'you totally led us astray here'. But *then*, just when you think that's it, the whole sky turns black, and there's all this thunder, and Indy gets this bad feeling, cos all these clouds are brewing and shit? So he says to Marion like, Don't look at it, you know? Like, keep your eyes shut no matter what, cos it's all gonna kick off.
So they shut their eyes, and it all goes quiet for a bit and it's all tense, but then suddenly all these blue ghosts start coming out of the ark, like weird kind of light ghosts, and they start floating around and the nazis are *loving* it, they're all like 'It's

bea*uuuu*tiful' and it's all mystical and nice, but *then*, one guy's
looking at a ghost thing and it turns from like a happy ghost
thing into like a *nasty* fucking ghost thing, and it pulls this face,
kind of like in Ghostbusters? And then *all* the ghosts turn bad,
and they start zapping all the hearts of the nazis and just *killing*
them, and the coat-hanger man is just screaming, and the
priest – or the head nazi I can't remember – his head just
fucking *explodes* – Like, and this is a *PG*! His head just explodes,
and the coat-hanger guy's head *melts* and all the nazis are just
getting fucking shanked by these ghosts, because they're like
the ghosts of God, you know?
And once everyone's dead, this big dust cloud thing flies up
and then sucks the lid back on and it's over – it's all silent. And
Indy's like, we're alright, don't worry, it's over now.
And then later, it cuts to, like, Indy back in America, and he's
back in his professor suit, and he's meeting with all these
corporate guys and he's pissed because he's like 'You've got to
destroy this ark, I saw a load of blue ghosts come out of it and
make dudes' heads explode' and they're just like 'Don't worry
about that, your job's done, leave us to deal with it' and
Marion's like 'Chill Indy, you've done all you can'. And you
think, what's gonna happen to the ark? But *then* it cuts to this
guy, like a janitor guy, wheeling the ark in a big box into this
warehouse, and you can see in the warehouse that there's like
millions of boxes, and this'll just be another one, and probably
everyone'll forget it's even there, so it's kind of a happy
ending, but it also makes you think, like, what's in those other
boxes, you know?
So it's kind of a mysterious ending.

. . .

Yeah?

Ollie   Yeah. I mean –

It's Raiders of the Lost Ark.

Zeppo   Yeah, that's what it's called. That's the film.

Ollie   Yeah. I've um – I've seen it.

Zeppo   Oh.

I thought you hadn't seen it.

Ollie   No, I've, I've seen it. I think everyone's seen it.

Zeppo   Oh.

Pause.

Ollie   Mr Zeppo –

Zeppo   Do you remember in the second one, where there's this guy, there's like this cult, and this guy with a big hat with horns on who rips dudes' hearts out?

Ollie   Mr Zeppo, do you think –

Zeppo   D'ywan a chicken nugger?

Ollie   N-no thank you.

Zeppo   I got a hundred.

Ollie   I'm fine.

Zeppo   The first time I drove up and said 'Can I have a hundred chicken nuggers' they were like 'Don't be a dick' but I was like 'Serious. One hundred.' And they make 'em for you.

I get a hundred every night.

Ollie   That's –

Zeppo   Hey,

Pass one of those from that sack back there.

Ollie *looks in a sack at her feet.*

It's full of Rubik's Cubes.

Ollie   One of these?

Zeppo   Pass one right back there.

She passes it back to the **Figure***, who starts solving it rapidly.*

Zeppo   What's your name again?

Ollie   Ollie –

Zeppo   Ollie?

Ollie   Yeah –

Zeppo   Like Oliver?

Ollie   Yes –

Zeppo   Like a boy's name?

Ollie   Yeah –

Zeppo   And what do you want?

Ollie   I came to – I need some – Help.

Zeppo   You need help from me?

Ollie   Yes, I –

Zeppo   Pass another one.

The **Figure** *has finished.* **Ollie** *passes another cube back.*

Zeppo   Someone told you to come find me.

Ollie   They said you know everyone and you know everything that happens –

Zeppo   They told you where I was.

Ollie   They said to wait on that flyover at night and you'd pick me up.

Zeppo   And I did.

Ollie   You did.

Zeppo   So here we are.

Ollie   Yeah –

Zeppo   And you want some help.

Ollie   Yes –

Zeppo   Pass another one back.

Ollie *does.*

Zeppo   So what do you need?

Ollie   My sister –

Zeppo   Your sister.

Ollie   I lost her. She's lost.

Zeppo   You lost your sister.

Ollie   She's missing.

Zeppo   She's a missing sister.

Ollie   She came here – She came here, to, to, Manchester, a few months ago, I don't know, I know she came here –

Zeppo   And she's gone.

Ollie   Yes.

Zeppo   She came here and now she's gone.

Ollie *nods.*

Zeppo   Well that's a job for the police, yeah? Pass another one.

She does.

Ollie   I don't – I think she went –

They said I can trust you –

Zeppo   Who said this?

Ollie   The person –

Zeppo   The *person*?

Ollie   The person who told me about you –

Zeppo   They said you can trust me?

Ollie   They said you would help without – Without asking any questions.

Zeppo   That's not the same as trust.

Ollie   No, I know, but –

Zeppo   I actually would totally *not* trust someone who asked no questions.

Ollie   No, but –

Zeppo   *You* don't want any questions.

Ollie   No.

Zeppo   You want dis*cretion*.

Ollie   She was involved in some –

Zeppo   Your sister?

Ollie   Yes, she was –

Zeppo   She was into some bad stuff you think.

Ollie   I think – Yes.

Zeppo   And now she's missing.

Ollie   And I think she's missing because she did something –

Or –

. . .

I don't think I can go to the police.

Pause.

Zeppo   Do you know who I am?

Ollie   You're like a, a, property guy.

Zeppo   I own a lot of the city.

Ollie   Yeah, they said – They said you owned the city.

Zeppo   A lot of it. A lot of what's inside this ring road. Commercial, industrial – Not residential. Except city centre. Only city centre residential.

Ollie   They said you're involved in everything –

Zeppo   Nah.

Ollie   No?

Zeppo   I don't get involved.

Ollie   But –

Zeppo   I just own everything. It's not good to get in*volved* in everything.

My dad owned the city before me, you know what happened to him?

Ollie   Your dad –

Zeppo   They nailed him to a brick wall with a steel rod through his face.

Ollie   Oh – God –

Zeppo   Right here. Through here.

Ollie   I'm sorry –

Zeppo   You know why that happened to him?

Ollie   Because – He got involved?

Zeppo   He got in*volved*. He owned everything so he thought he would start getting involved in everything, and you know what happens when you get involved?

What happened?

Ollie   He got a, a steel –

Zeppo   Steel rod through the head. Right here. Through his *face*.

So I don't *get* involved. I'm *neutral*. I'm a very neutral person. I rent my land and my buildings out to *everyone*. To *anyone*. I don't pick favourites. I don't ask questions, like you said. You know what the most important ethos is for today's turbulent times?

Ollie   I – What?

Zeppo   Selective education.

Ollie   Selective –

Zeppo   Selective education. You know what that means?

Ollie   That you choose –

Zeppo   You choose what you educate yourself about. That doesn't just apply to me and my business, that's *everyone*. That's a big decision *everyone* needs make. About *every*thing.

Ollie   B –

Zeppo   Like these chicken nuggers, yeah? I fucking love 'em. I fucking *love* chicken nuggers.

I eat 'em every night.

I drive round this fucking ring road all night, I take my meetings in my car, I solve problems, I do business, I eat nuggers. Mc*Donald's* chicken nuggers.

*Mc*Nuggers.

They're the *best* – The batter? No other nugger compares. Accept no substitutes.

But maybe one day I'm thinking, hey, how do they make the nuggers?

And if this was twenty years ago or whatever I'd have to go and like, *find* a guy to tell me how they make them. I'd have to make phone calls. Drive places. Ask around. Probably I wouldn't bother, because I don't care that much. Back then you only looked into things you actually cared about, cos it was *effort*.

But now? I can find out in like three seconds.

Ollie   About the nuggers.

Zeppo   About the nuggers. I can just type that shit into my *phone* and I'll know. Immediately.

But let me ask you this man, do you think if I look into the nuggers, if I open that door, am I gonna find out like, positive things? Or am I gonna maybe find out horrible things about how they turn a chicken into this? Do you think maybe if I look it up, I'm not gonna wanna eat nuggers anymore?

Ollie   Well –

Zeppo   What do you think man? Option 1? Or B?

Ollie   The second one, probably.

Zeppo   Course the fucking second one! Course!

I want to eat these. So I don't open that door. You know?

Ollie   Yeah, I guess –

Zeppo   You gotta pick and choose what you *give* a shit about.

Now it's so fucking easy to look everything up, we get to see what's holding the walls up, you know? But this is not a good idea because inevitably? In*vari*ably? Every part of our lives and culture and diet and health and the clothes we wear and the music we like and the films we watch and the friends we have and all of this – you go deep enough, you'll find all this *stuff*, the detritus of our lives, it's all built on this foundation of pain and shit and suffering. It's like it's impossible to be a good person now. You can't *be* a good person any more. There's no such thing. There's just people who are *aware* of the pain they're causing, and people who *aren't* aware.

That's why I don't get involved with who rents my buildings. I don't know what happens in them. I don't *want* to know.

Knowledge is a *responsibility.*

And some of these people,

These are bad people, the people I deal with.

But I don't pick and choose – I deal with *everyone.*

My dad just deals with *some* people, but then those people move on, or they get killed, and suddenly you're on a side, you didn't even know there *was* sides, but you're *on* one, and now doors are open and your eyes are open and what happens?

Ollie   Steel –

Zeppo   *BAM!* Steel rod through the head.

So I'm neutral, man. I'm a very neutral person. I don't *get* involved.

I just sit outside, and watch everyone going round and round.

I sit outside and I fa*cilitate,* and I *watch.*

Some people can do that.

It's like a form of time travel.

. . .

Pass one of those back.

She does.

Ollie   Mr Zeppo, does this – I mean – I don't want to be rude –

Zeppo   Not at all, man.

Ollie   I was just wondering how that relates? To my sister?

Zeppo   . . .

Is it a good idea to go looking for her?

Pause.

Ollie   . . .

I have to find her –

Zeppo   Why?

Ollie   Because she's –

She's my sister.

. . .

I can't just – Abandon her –

I can't stop thinking about it. About where she is. Or what happened, or –

I have these nightmares about it. About things happening to her.

And I wake up with all these cuts all over me like I'm clawing at myself in my sleep –

Zeppo   And you think if you follow that road, it's gonna lead you somewhere good?

I'm telling you, man.

There are doors.

And there are *doors*.

And then you're involved.

And people who get involved, they get steel rods through the head.

Or they disappear.

Beat.

Pass another one.

She does.

Pause.

Ollie   I have money, I can –

Zeppo   I don't need money.

Ollie   But –

Zeppo   I don't need money. I have too much money.

Ollie   But – What do you –

. . .

I don't know . . .

Pause.

Zeppo   I like you man, do you like me?

Ollie   Yeah – Yes – I mean – You talk kind of strange –

Zeppo   Most nights it's just the same,

over and over,

can I have some money,

can I have this building or whatever,

you know,

boring man,

and then you're here and it's like, we can actually have a conver*sation*, you know?

Ollie *smiles.*

Zeppo   You're nervous though, you're a nervous person man, do you think?

Ollie   Maybe, yes, probably, my – my sister's the confident one.

That's probably why she, you know –

. . .

Pause.

Zeppo   People are disappearing.

. . .

Ollie   . . . What?

Zeppo   . . .

I hear a lot of talk about people disappearing.

. . .

It's something people are talking about.

. . .

Hand another one back there.

Ollie *does.*

Pause.

Zeppo   Have you heard of Pomona?

Ollie   Pomona?

Zeppo   Do you know where it is?

Ollie   N – It's a place?

Zeppo   It's an island.

Concrete island.

Here.

Right in the middle of town.

Strip of land with the canal on both sides.

Tram tracks and train tracks and roads all surrounding it.

There's one road in and out and it's gated at both ends.

Nothing there but cracked asphalt and weeds.

All overgrown.

Street lights don't work.

It's a hole.

A hole in the middle of the city.

Looks like what the world'll be in a few thousand years.

Ollie   Do you own it?

Zeppo   I own it.

Ollie   Why's there nothing there?

Zeppo   Because I get paid to leave it like that.

They want it like that. These people.

No reason for anyone to go there.

Ollie   Who rents it from you?

Zeppo   . . .

Pause.

Zeppo   Lot of talk about people disappearing.

Pomona's a place that finds itself in those conversations.

I don't know why.

But if you're looking for someone lost.

. . .

Might be a place to look.

Ollie   Thank y –

Zeppo   But listen.

. . .

I don't recommend it.

. . .

You know?

. . .

I don't recommend it.

. . .

Pause.

Pass another one back.

Ollie *does.*

The **Figure** *solves it.*

/two.

Fay *is in a phonebox.*
Rainsoaked and muddied.
Rain hammers.
She hugs a laptop.

She picks up the receiver.

Pause.

Hangs up.

Pause.

Picks it up again.

Dials 999.

Pause.

Hangs up.

A car passes –

She crouches/shields her face.

Pause.

She picks it up and dials another number.

Pause.

Fay   Stacy –

No –

. . .

Yes –

Can you –

. . .

I'm going to be late back.

. . .

I don't know what time, I'm just –

. . .

I –

I don't know –

Why is she still up?

She should be in bed –

Put her to bed –

No –

No –

I'll pay you for the –

I will *pay* you extra Stacy, you just have to stay –

Because I *can't*. I can't get *home* now –

. . .

Later. I don't know – Stacy, listen –

Listen –

Listen to me –

Don't answer the phone tonight.

. . .

No.

No.

Not for *any*one –

Because I told you –

Because I'm *telling* you –

And don't answer the door.

Don't answer the door to anyone who knocks, whoever knocks, don't –

. . .

No –

I *told* you you couldn't have him round –

. . .

No –

No,

No,

Listen –

No,

Stacy,

Stacy shut the fuck up and *listen* to me –

Do *not* answer the door,

Do *not* answer the phone,

Put her to bed, close the curtains, lock the doors and windows –

Because I'm *telling* you to –

Keaton *knocks on the glass.*

Fay *jumps/shouts.*

Fay   *Jesus* –

What?!

(*Into the phone.*) Hold *on* Stacy –

Keaton *stares.*

Fay   I'm on the *phone.*

What do you want?

What do you *want?!*

/three.

Gale *is leaning against a locked door, pouring bottles of pills into her mouth, on the phone.*

Gale   Yes I'm still on hold, I'm holding – I shouldn't have to – I shouldn't *be* on fucking hold –

. . .

. . .

Yes – Listen –

Yes –

. . .

Yes.

I told you the password already, I shouldn't –

Yes. Will you listen?

I want you to take –

Yes –

I want you to take the money, all the money, from my account –

Take all of the money from the account –

Yes –

All of it –

Take it out, take it out and stack it up – Put it in a pile, a pile –

I want you to pile it up in the street –

In the *street* –

Yes –

I want you to pile it up and I want you to *burn* it, understand?

. . .

Yes.

Yes.

I want you to make a big pile of it in the street and burn it.

All of it.

And if you can do that in front of a, a, food bank, or a homeless shelter, or, or *something* –

. . .

Because I'm asking you –

. . .

Because it's my money –

. . .

Because I'm *telling* you –

. . .

Because I hired the *fucking* Marx Brothers –

Because you cannot trust *anyone* to do *anything* and *everyone* is a *fucking* moron and they won't take me down there –

They won't take me!

I fucked up and she told me, I saw her and she told me if I fucked up and I *fucked* up so they're coming and they're here and no one gets out, *no one gets out* from down there but they won't, they won't take me, *no one* takes me, you can't take a *corpse*, you can't take me if I took *myself* already and I'm taking all the money they can't have the money, take the money –

DON'T YOU *FUCKING* DARE PUT ME ON HOLD AGAIN CRAIG –

. . .

You calm down –

You calm down Craig –

You are *paid* –

You are *paid* to do what I –

It's *my* money –

You fucking –

It's *MINE* –

What is the use in having an account manager if you won't manage my accounts the way I fucking *want* –

. . .

BURN IT. In the *STREET*. *BURN IT*.

Screams and noise outside. Shouting.

Gale *stuffs more pills in.*

Gale   Are you *listening* to me?

Hammering on the door.

(*To the door.*) Fuck yourself!

Hammering on the door.

Fuck yourself!

/four.

Charlie *and* **Moe** *under a bridge.*

Wet, dark, cars overhead.

Moe   Come on.

Charlie   I don't –

Moe   Come *on*.

Charlie   There must be – Maybe we don't –

Moe *hits him.*

Moe   Come *on*.

Charlie   I can't –

Moe *hits him again.*

Moe   Do it.

Charlie   Stop –

Again.

Charlie *hits him back.*

Moe   That's shite. Harder.

Charlie   That's as hard as – That hurt –

Moe   Fucking –

He lies down on the floor.

Here. Kick me.

Charlie   No –

Moe   *Kick me.*

Here.

Kick me *here.*

Charlie *kicks his face.*

Moe   Again.

Charlie *kicks again.*

Moe   There. Blood. Better.

Charlie   That's enough . . .

Moe   This is the story, this is how it happened –

Charlie   That's enough now –

Moe   There were other people, they hurt us, she got away –
Take this –

Charlie   No –

Moe   Put it – Take it – Close your – *Hold* it. Put it in my side. Here.

Charlie   I'm not doing this –

Moe   If you don't then that's the end of us, alright?

Last chance.

It has to look real and it has to look bad.

Pause.

Moe   *Do* it.

Charlie *stabs him.*

Charlie   Are you okay –

Moe   Again. My leg.

Charlie   No –

Moe   *Do* it.

Charlie *stabs his leg.*

Blood.

Moe   There. Okay.

Charlie   I have to be sick.

Moe   Give me that.

Charlie   I feel –

Moe *punches* **Charlie**.

Moe   Hold still.

Again.

Again.

Again.

Charlie   Stop it – Stop –

Again.

Again.

Moe *stabs* **Charlie** *in the side.*

Again.

In his thigh.

Blood.

Lots of blood.

Moe   Stop, stop, that's it, that's it –

Charlie   Don't do any more . . .

Moe   That's it, it's all . . . Sit down. It's done – We're done –

Charlie *slumps to the floor.*

Pause.

Moe   Catch your breath.

Moe *throws the knife.*

Pause.

Charlie   It's bleeding a lot . . .

Moe   That's good, we want it – It has to.

Charlie   You weren't going to stop . . .

Moe   I stopped.

I stopped myself.

I wasn't –

. . .

I stopped.

. . .

Sit up.

Charlie   It's all – Moving –

Moe *looks.*

He's hit an artery.

Moe   Okay –

Charlie   It's all coming out.

Moe   Stand up.

Charlie   No . . .

Moe   Grab me and stand up.

Charlie   . . . shut up . . .

Moe   *Just* – . . . wait –

He takes his shirt off and wraps it around **Charlie***'s leg.*

Moe   Hold that.

Charlie   . . . no . . .

Moe   Hold it tight like this. Like this.

Like *this*.

Charlie   stop yelling at me . . .

Moe   I'll phone an, an ambulance.

Charlie   . . . no –

Moe   Yes –

Charlie   The Girl –

Moe   That's not – She won't – This is better, this makes it look more –

. . .

. . .

Fuck.

Pause.

Cars overhead.

Charlie   we messed everything up . . .

Moe   We're going to fix it –

Charlie   . . . buh . . .

Moe   What?

Charlie   . . . it's better . . .

Moe   Hold it tight. *Hold* it. Let me think.

Charlie   . . . fuh . . .

Moe   Sit up. Sit *up*.

Charlie   . . .

Moe   . . . Sit up.

. . .

Come on.

Wake up.

Sit up.

Wake up.

Hey.

Hey.

. . .

. . .

Pause.

Cars overhead.

Moe *sits down in a heap next to* **Charlie**.

Pause.

He holds his hand.

Cars overhead.

/five.

Fay *and* **Ollie**.

Fay   This is your room.

Ollie   Okay.

Fay   You can do stuff to it if you wanna – If you wanna *hang* – I don't know –

Ollie   Decorate.

Fay   You can decorate it. If you want to.

Ollie   It's fine like this.

Fay   Well you just have to ask Gale. If you want to.

Ollie   If I want to mess with the . . . the *vibe* . . .

Fay   . . . Yeah.

Pause.

Ollie   The TV –

Fay   It doesn't have channels.

Ollie   It's just –

Fay   There's a thing of DVDs –

Sometimes they might want to watch something –

Ollie   In the background.

Fay   Or they're nervous or whatever.

Ollie   Help the *mood* . . .

Fay   Most of them are pretty scratched.

Ollie   And that's a camera.

Fay   Yeah.

Ollie   In case –

Fay   In case one of them tries to hurt you.

Ollie   *Has* anyone ever –

Fay   Before I started here some guy cut this girl's face up with a bottle.

Ollie   Ugh –

Fay   Yeah.

Ollie   Jesus.

Fay   I don't remember her name but he cut her nose half off.

Ollie   Fuck.

Fay   So that's why the camera.

Ollie   Obviously, yeah.

Fay   I mean they just watch you.

Ollie   They watch you?

Fay   The guys who check the cameras.

Ollie   They just sit and watch?

Fay   Yeah. Don't go in that room. It stinks of cum.

Ollie   What?

Fay   It really does.

Beat.

Fay   Oh, and there's the red button under the nightstand.

Ollie   The nightstand –

Fay   The little – This thing, the table next to the bed.

Ollie   Okay.

Fay   You press the button and, you know, alarms.

Ollie   Right.

Fay   And in there are also things of lube and toys and wipes. Stuff like that.

Ollie   Okay.

Beat.

Fay   It's a lot safer than other places. That's what they all say anyway.

The ones who worked other places.

Ollie *nods.*

Fay   Did they tell you everything else?

Ollie   Yeah, um –

Fay   They just told me to show you the room.

Ollie   No, yeah, thank you.

Fay   My main tip is just to make sure they shower first – They don't technically *have* to but I always insist. And if they don't want to I'll maybe – Like I'll take my top off, and that usually – Usually they take one after that.

Ollie   Right.

Fay   Because they're pretty good showers here, they're strong, so it'll scoosh away most bad smells, or bits of food or whatever.

Ollie   Bits of *food*?

Fay   My first week here some guy had a lump of chicken in his pubes.

Ollie   *What?*

Fay   Yeah, just sort of – *nestled*. Nestled in there.

Ollie   When did you find –

Fay   I was going down on him and I thought it kind of smelt really, you know, bad –

Worse than the usual bad.

And then I saw this weird –

Like I thought it was some kind of tumour, or –

Ollie   Ugh!

Fay   Yeah. It was bad.

Ollie   Blegh.

Fay   Yeah.

Beat.

Ollie   So showers, then.

Pause.

Fay   So I'm just, like – I'm two doors down.

Ollie   Do you know –

Beat.

Fay   What?

Beat.

Ollie   Do you –

Are there ways to sort of make . . .

To increase your pay, or –

. . .

Fay   Um. You can just do stuff – Do more stuff that the others – *wouldn't* do –

Ollie   Yeah – And I guess –

Do you ever –

Make, uh, *films*, or –

Fay   No.

Ollie   No.

Beat.

Fay   Some of the others have. I don't do that.

Ollie   Okay.

Fay   Maybe talk to them about that.

Ollie   Okay.

. . .

And –

Fay –

Sorry –

Do you know where I can maybe –

(*Coughs.*)

Where I can get some, uh –

I mean, I already –

But maybe you know where the *better* sort of –

Fay   I don't do that.

Ollie   No, sure.

Fay   I don't know about that.

Ollie   Yeah.

Beat.

Ollie   Sorry.

Fay   Gale doesn't like that. Don't let her know that's –

Ollie   I won't – I don't even –

It's fine.

Thanks.

Thank you.

Beat.

Fay   'Kay.

Pause.

Ollie   What happened to the girl in here before?

Fay   She's gone.

Ollie   She got fired, or . . . ?

Beat.

Ollie   What?

Fay   . . .

Her boyfriend came looking for her cos she didn't come home.

But she wasn't here.

She's gone.

Beat.

Ollie   Oh.

Beat.

Fay   She's the second one that happened to.

/six.

Keaton *and* **Charlie**.

Charlie   . . .

Are you here for –

Did you see my flyer?

. . . Are you here for Dungeons and Dragons?

Pause.

Keaton *nods.*

Charlie   Cool.

Well.

You're the first right now,

Maybe some more will come in a sec,

But actually this is like week four and you're the first person who's *ever* come, so probably not actually.

. . .

You sure have a lot of expensive stuff.

. . .

You just walk around with everything on show like that?

She looks down at herself.

Charlie   I bet even those trainers are worth like a hundred.

Keaton   Two hundred.

Charlie   *Two* hundred. Whoa. That's a lot of money to spend on trainers.

I don't think even all my clothes together add up to two hundred.

Like, what I'm wearing right now. The whole lot.

Do you have a good job?

Do you have a job that pays a lot?

Sorry, that's rude.

Keaton   I have a lot of money.

Charlie   Yeah, it looks it.

Sorry, I'm being rude.

My job pays pretty well, but I spend all my money on comics and things like that.

Keaton   You like comics.

Charlie   Yeah, I'm a collector. I'm kind of a hoarder.

I can show you later if you like.

I actually have some quite rare items.

Beat.

Keaton   What's your job.

Charlie   I'm a kind of a uh – security guard.

Keaton   You're small.

Charlie   Yeah. I don't really – It's not really a physical job? It's more just a standing-all-day job.

. . .

Have you ever played D and D before?

Keaton   No.

Charlie   Well that's okay, I can teach you.

Though I should warn you, we'll be playing a different kind of game than usual – I write the games myself, so it's not a standard RPG experience.

Do you know what an RPG is?

Keaton   No.

Charlie   It means role playing game. That's what the game is. I can teach you everything. It's not hard. Actually, I should say it's not hard to learn, but it's hard to *master*.

Pause.

How come you fancied coming to my club?

Keaton *shrugs.*

Charlie   You just want to meet people maybe?

Keaton   Yes.

Charlie   Well I hear that. I find it very difficult to meet new people and make friends.

Especially in a city.

That's the main part of the reason why I started this club.

Keaton   You don't have any friends.

Charlie   I have like – I have a friend through work.

Keaton   You have one friend.

Charlie   Yeah. What about you?

Keaton *shakes head.*

Charlie   You don't have any friends?

Keaton *shakes head.*

Charlie   Wow. And I thought I was bad! Don't worry though, we're gonna make friends now. You can't help but make friends with people when you're playing RPGs. It's a very social experience.

Even though there's only two of us.

Do you wanna sit?

I can start explaining the game now.

They sit.

Charlie   Do you want something to eat or drink?

Keaton *shakes head.*

Charlie   Well let me know if you do, and I can go get us something. I have lemonade and crisps and stuff. And dip.

Okay.

So the game we're going to play is one I wrote myself, it's called 'Cthulhu Awakens'. It's a Lovecraftian game. Do you know H.P. Lovecraft?

Keaton *shakes head.*

Charlie   Well, he's a writer who wrote horror and science-fiction stories.

I can lend you a book to take home.

Basically, I've based the game on several characters and concepts in his stories, mainly the character of *Cthulhu*.

Cthulhu is like a big, giant monster thing, with an octopus head. He looks like this, see? He's cool, isn't he?

He's actually an evil god. And in the stories he's one of the 'Great Old Ones', which are – Are you still following me?

Keaton *nods.*

Charlie   The 'Great Old Ones' are the beasts that ruled the earth before we did. 'Cept they've been asleep now for aeons. That's basically like a long, long time. They're actually sort of a metaphor for the universe's apathy for us and the meaningless nature of life, but that's not important for the game.

That's just context.

Throughout the game, you'll come into contact with a cult who are trying to awaken Cthulhu, to begin a new dark reign of chaos (don't worry, that's not a spoiler), and your task is to prevent this from happening.

Do you understand?

Keaton   Where's the board.

Charlie   Ah, you see, this isn't like a normal board game, yeah? The board is actually our *imagination*.

Keaton   I have to beat you.

Charlie   No, it's a cooperative game in the sense that I tell the story and present you with options, and you decide which options to take. Whether you succeed or not is decided by rolling dice, like in a normal game, 'cept these dice have a lot more sides, see? Do you get it?

Keaton   No.

Charlie   Well don't worry, you'll pick it up as we go.

Shall we start?

Keaton   Okay.

Charlie   It's going to be fun, promise.

Here's your character sheet, this is like your stats for how good you are at things.

What's your name?

Keaton   Keaton.

Charlie   Keaton? That's a cool name. I won't even change that. You can be called Keaton in the game, that'll make it more immersive.

I'm Charlie, nice to meet you.

Are you ready?

Keaton   Okay.

Charlie   Here we go. You are standing alone on a crowded street. People push past you as if you're not there. It's a cold and lonely city, and you're not here by choice. You've come here to search for your sister, who came here some weeks ago, but has disappeared under mysterious circumstances. An anonymous phone call you received at your hotel told you to head to a tavern called 'The Palace'. Shall we head there now?

Keaton   Okay.

/seven.

Charlie *rolls a dice.*

Charlie   You are walking through a shopping centre

Keaton   You are walking

Ollie   I am walking through a shopping centre – it has a name but I forgot –

– You're struck by how sterile it is and how
– isolated you feel.
– The whole centre is a loop
– A circuit
– if you set off walking eventually
– you end up back where you were,
– but you might not realise because all the shops look the same
– big, strip-lit, colourful
– shuttered
– steel barns

- They could decide one day
- to close all the shutters
- but keep the centre open,

Ollie   and I bet people would just keep walking and walking and walking

- round and round and round
- looking for
- an open shop without even realising they were doing
- loops.
- It's hard to recognise when your life is looping.
- You are walking.

Ollie   I am walking

- the loop
- not thinking sort of thinking

Ollie   about my sister

- about the man
- the man in the car
- the road around the city
- what he told you
- and
- it's getting dark outside
- because the nights are drawing in
- it's dark early

Ollie   and I'm just

- walking
- and walking
- and walking
- and

Ollie   glancing at the other people shopping

- or walking
- thinking about your sister
- about the man
- about the hole

- the hole at the heart of the city
- You pass a lot of people
- None of them look at you
- All stare straight ahead as they loop

Ollie   then at some point on my

- maybe
- eighth loop
- maybe
- you notice

Ollie   I notice this woman staring at me.

- The woman is stood
- She's stood just outside a shoe shop and she's holding
- She's clutching
- a laptop
- no bags
- nothing
- she hasn't bought anything
- that you can see
- and her face is contorted,
- twisted
- up in this expression of horror,
- real horror
- real terror
- as if she's just seen
- the face of God
- or some unimaginable sight

Ollie   And I stop walking

- You stop walking
- and look at her

Ollie   we're looking at each other

- she looks at you
- and all the other
- shoppers and
- people

Ollie   are passing between us,

–   You're looking

Ollie   we're looking through the bustle of everyone.

–   And she moves
–   She comes over

Ollie   She pushes through the people

–   The sea of people
–   The loop
–   She pushes through the loop
–   Like she knows you
–   To hiss
–   To whisper

Ollie   To spit

–   Like she knows you
–   Eyes flash fire and black
–   Something about leaving
–   Something about gone

Ollie   Something about They

–   They took you
–   She said
–   She thought
–   I thought
–   You let me
–   They're coming
–   She told me
–   I told her

Ollie   She's threatened

–   She threatens
–   Her hands are on you
–   Pulling at you
–   Louder

Ollie   She's louder

- She spits
- She's screaming
- Something about they
- Heads turn
- She pulls you down
- Down
- Screaming
- Down
- the other shoppers turn
- Heads turn

Ollie   Heads turn to look at us

- At this woman
- The screaming woman
- And more hands
- Hands on her
- Pull at her
- The loop stops
- They come to help you
- You're surprised

Ollie   They pull at her

- Hands on her
- Pulling at her
- She scrambles for the laptop

Ollie   She bolts,

- She's gone
- she's *gone*.
- A ghost.
- The shoppers move away
- They leave
- They continue

Ollie   And I'm left there

- not knowing what
- She broke the loop

Ollie   she broke my flow of looping and thinking

—   The others push
—   push

Ollie   the others push past me as I stand

—   You stand
—   Frozen
—   The loop fractures
—   But continues.

/eight.

Charlie *and* **Moe.**

Charlie *drools long ropes of spit onto the floor.*

Moe   Stop that.

Charlie   I'm trying to do that thing – Where you –

Moe   Stop it.

Charlie   Where you make like a long line of spit all the way down then you, you *suck* it back up again –

Moe   Don't.

Pause.

Stop it.

Charlie   Do you want to know what my fetish is?

Moe   No.

Charlie   It's weird.

Moe   I don't want to know.

Charlie   I have this –

Moe   I don't want to hear.

Charlie   – this real desire to jizz on everything.

Moe   . . .

Charlie   Like this,

this sort of,

this *urge*,

like I want to cover the whole city in my jizz.

(*Laughs.*) Isn't that weird?!

Moe   Yes.

Charlie   I think about it all the time, about how I could make everything in the whole city have this thin film of my jizz over everything, y'know?

Moe   I don't know.

Charlie   It doesn't even feel like a *sexual* thing, like I don't think it's a sex thing, it doesn't turn me on when I think about it –

Moe   Please.

Charlie   It's not a fetish. It's like this *urge*. Like needing a piss or something, like I just *need* to do it. Even you. I even want to put my jizz on you.

Moe   Stop.

Charlie   But yeah, not in a sex way. It wouldn't be sexy.

Do you know how I first found out I wanted to do this?

When I was really young, like before I even started masturbating properly, but I was still getting boners, we lived near this hospital, and round the back of the hospital was this mattress there with a hole in it, like it was all sponge you know? So I would go and lie down on this mattress and fuck it.

(*Laughs.*) This was when I was like eleven or twelve or something so I didn't really get what I was doing but I just used to put my dick in things all the time. And when I found that mattress I would just go there all the time and put my dick in it and fuck it until all my jizz would come out and soak into the sponge. After a while the sponge got all crusty. Isn't that gross?

Moe   . . .

Charlie   Then this one time, the mattress, it was round the back of the hospital, under this window, and I used to like, crouch, like I'd *sneak* under the window so they wouldn't see, so I could fuck the mattress. So then this one time I actually took a look in the window, like after I'd jizzed already, and it was basically this room – I don't know what they had wrong with them or anything – But it was this room full of people all sat in these chairs with all wires and stuff coming out of them, all tubes, and they were mostly old people, and it was like a kind of a ward, except there was not often any nurses in there or anything, just these people sat in the chairs with all the tubes and wires. And they all looked at me. I don't know if they were like, cancer guys or that thing – what's that thing with kidneys?

Moe   Dialysis.

Charlie   Dialysis. Maybe they were that. Cos of all the wires.

They were something, anyway.

And when I looked at them – they all had really sad faces, 'cept this one lady who smiled and waved at me, I guess cos I was a little boy, and old ladies like little boys – but when I looked at them I just for some reason really wanted to like, *jizz* on their faces. I just felt like that was something I should do.

And not in some horrible sex way or anything, but like for some reason I thought it might help them or make them better or something.

Because I knew about sperms, and sperms are basically like a lifeforce, aren't they?

So maybe I thought if I jizzed on all their faces, all the ill or dying people or whatever, they'd get better.

And ever since I had that thought I just basically wanted to jizz on everything.

. . .

Isn't that weird?

Moe   I don't want to hear this.

Charlie   I'm just trying to pass the time, conversation passes the time.

Moe   That's not a conversation. That's just you telling me about your dick.

Charlie   It wasn't really about my dick, it was about my jizz.

Moe   Fine.

Charlie   It was more about my balls than anything.

Moe   Okay.

Charlie   What do you think the psychology behind that is?

Moe   I don't know.

Charlie   That maybe I think my balls have healing properties?

Moe   I don't know.

Charlie   Because balls are like the life-givers?

Moe   I don't care about any of this.

Charlie   I think probably Freud would have something to say about it.

He goes back to spitting.

Moe   This is her now. Stop.

Enter **Gale**.

Charlie *tries to suck his spit back up but fails and spits down his front.*

Moe   Sorry.

Charlie   I didn't mean to −

Gale   Have they been today?

Moe   No.

Charlie   I like your car −

Gale   No one's been?

Moe   / No.

Charlie   It's a very expensive-looking car. I imagine Tom Cruise would drive a car like that. Or Jesus. If Jesus lived today he might drive a car like that.

Gale   Make him stop talking to me.

Charlie   Sorry −

Gale   Make him stop talking to me or I'll punch him in the throat.

Moe   Shut up.

Charlie   . . .

Gale   Thank you. You're Moe. That's your name. Your name is Moe, yes?

Moe   Yeah −

Gale   You're the serious one. He's the idiot, I remember. You're the serious one, aren't you.

Moe   I −

Gale   You are. In the double act of you. You're the serious one.

Moe   I don't −

Gale   Shut up. You are.

. . .

There is a person. A *woman* −

You're listening?

Moe   Yes –

Gale   There is a person who needs to not be around any more.

. . .

Yes?

Moe   . . .

Beat.

Gale   I have a photo, and I have a name, and this person has to not exist any more.

. . .

I want you to end this person. I want a full stop on this person.

I want you to make this person not alive any more.

That's layman's terms, yes?

Pause.

Charlie   We don't really do that –

. . .

We can't – We can't do that –

Gale   It's very simple.

Charlie   But –

Gale   It's very straightforward.

I'm asking you to do something, and you're going to do it.

. . .

You can throw her off a building, or wrap a wire round her neck, or, or, something –

I don't care, I don't mind how it's done. That's entirely up to you.

Moe   That's not what we do –

Gale   You do what I tell you to do.

Charlie   But –

Gale   You get paid a lot of money to stand here at this gate.

You get paid a lot more money than a job like this should pay.

Charlie   But –

Gale   Is this true?

Charlie   Yes but –

Gale   Didn't I *tell* you not to speak? Didn't I *tell* you?

Charlie   I –

Gale   I will put your eyes out. Believe me. Believe what I'm saying.

Moe   Shut up.

Pause.

Gale   This isn't optional. This isn't something you can opt out of.

I'm telling you to do it.

So you do it.

Moe   Are there not –

. . .

More experienced people.

. . .

Pause.

Gale   You do know about The Girl?

Beat.

Moe   . . . What girl?

Gale   *The* Girl. The girl that doesn't need a name in a city filled with girls.

Beat.

Charlie   She's a story.

She's like a, a, an urban myth.

Gale *takes a sheet of paper out of her pocket, balls it up, and drops it.*

Gale   Okay?

Charlie   The Girl's not a real – She's not a real thing.

Gale   Fast. Tonight.

She leaves.

Pause.

Charlie   She's not a real thing, is she Moe?

Pause.

She's like the monster under the bed or something.

She's not real.

Is she Moe.

. . .

She just said that to scare us.

Moe.

Pause.

Moe   . . . Pick it up.

/nine.

Fay *and* **Ollie**.

Ollie *is beaten and bloodied.*

Fay   Jesus –

Ollie   Can I –

Fay   What happened to you?

Pause.

Fay   What happened?

Ollie   I – I got mugged.

Fay   Where?

I mean –

Sit down. Sit –

Ollie   I'm fine –

Fay   Are you alright?

Ollie   I'm fine – It looks worse . . . than it is.

Fay   Where did this happen? Just outside?

Ollie   Yeah –

Fay   Just right outside?

Ollie   In an alley –

Fay   They pulled you into an alley?

Ollie   Yeah . . .

Fay   With knives?

Ollie   Yea – No – Just –

Fay   They hit you?

Ollie   I'm okay.

Fay   Have you called the police?

Ollie   No –

Fay   Do you want to –

Ollie   No.

Fay   You should probably –

Ollie   I don't *want* to.

. . .

They won't catch them anyway.

. . .

Happens every day.

Pause.

Fay   What did they take?

Ollie   . . .

Fay   Just money?

Ollie   Yeah –

Fay   Your card? Did they take your card?

Ollie   Yes.

Fay   We should call the bank then –

Ollie   What?

Fay   We have to call the bank, to cancel the card –

Ollie   No –

Fay   That stops them taking more –

Ollie   I already – Did that.

I did that already.

Beat.

Ollie   Can I – I just came in here to borrow some of the –

The wipe things.

I used mine.

. . .

They have alcohol in I think, or –

Fay   Here.

Ollie   Thank you.

Pause.

Fay   Was it just one guy?

Ollie   No.

Fay   Was it –

Ollie   I don't really –

Fay   Sorry.

Ollie   I don't want to talk about it.

Pause.

Fay   You look terrible.

Ollie   Thank you.

Fay   No, I mean –

Ollie   I know.

Fay   I don't think they'll let you work like this.

Ollie   What?

Fay   I don't think you can.

Ollie   . . . Christ.

She cries a little, tries to hide it.

Pause.

Fay   Did you really . . .

Ollie   What.

Fay   . . .

I don't think –

You didn't get –

Get mugged.

Did you.

Pause.

Ollie   . . .

Fay   It's okay, you don't have to –

You know.

Pause.

Ollie   . . .

I made a film.

Pause.

Fay   You made a film?

Pause.

Oh.

Pause.

Ollie   . . .

Four of them –

Kicked me round this basement for a while.

. . .

It was like a rape –

A rape thing.

That was the story. Of the film.

Pause.

Fay   Oh.

Pause.

Ollie   Embarrassed.

Fay   No – It's –

. . .

Pause.

Fay   You got – You got paid a lot?

Ollie   . . .

not enough.

. . .

Beat.

Fay   Do you owe someone money?

Ollie   . . .

Fay   How much?

Ollie   . . . too much to pay back.

Fay   What do you owe it for?

Ollie   . . .

Fay   Can you – Can you just run away?

Ollie   They find you. They find everybody.

Beat.

Fay   What about – Do you have any family?

Ollie   . . . I have a sister . . .

Fay   A sister –

Ollie   I have a twin sister . . .

Fay   Okay, can we call her?

Ollie   I don't know where she is . . .

Fay   Well what's her name?

Ollie   . . . Ollie.

Fay   Ollie? Like Oliver? Like a boy's name?

Ollie *nods.*

Fay Where do you think she is?

Ollie I don't know. Here, maybe.

Fay In Manchester?

Ollie Maybe I don't.

Fay Don't what?

Ollie Maybe I don't have one.

Beat.

I think I have one, I feel like I have a sister –

I can remember seeing myself places I haven't been to.

She looks just like me.

But maybe I don't.

Fay I – Are you okay? Do you feel –

Ollie I think she came here looking for me.

Fay Well –

Ollie I think she came here to find me . . .

Fay Well let's look her up and –

Ollie I don't want to involve her.

Fay You need –

Ollie I don't want to involve her.

. . .

I'm bleeding all over your –

Fay It's fine.

Ollie I'm such a fuck-up.

Fay It's okay.

Ollie You ran away, didn't you?

Beat.

Ollie   They told me. The others. About your husband.

. . .

He's in the police.

. . .

Did he ever find you?

Beat.

Fay   Not yet.

Ollie   They said you're saving up to leave –

Fay   I don't want to talk about that. That's not important now –

Ollie   I would have cut his face off.

. . .

When he was sleeping.

Peeled it off.

Pause.

Ollie   Do you hate everyone you fuck here?

Fay   Why don't we –

Ollie   Do you hate them? All the men who come here.

Pause.

Fay   No.

I used to think so.

I don't *like* most of them.

. . .

But not hate.

Ollie   I do.

I hate all of them.

I think I hate everyone.

It's like a sickness I can feel in my guts.

I wake up every morning and I feel it all over.

I can't get to sleep because it turns in me.

All this hate.

I think I'd sleep a lot easier if I knew none of us would wake up tomorrow.

Do you feel that?

. . .

One day I'll come back to this city on fire.

I'll have flames pouring from me.

And I'll keep walking through the streets in circles until everyone and everything is just ash.

I'll bring the end to everyone.

Pause.

Ollie   Can you promise me something?

Fay   . . . what?

Ollie   If I go missing like the others.

Don't come looking for me.

. . .

I hope no one comes looking.

/ten.

Charlie and **Moe** *in a car. Stationary. Rain.*
Silence.

Charlie *gets a Gameboy out and starts playing*

Pause.

Moe   Turn that off.

Charlie   Why?

Moe   We're working.

Charlie   Can I show you my Pokemons?

Moe   Turn it off.

He does.

Pause.

Charlie   We just wait here –

Moe   You have the photo, you know what she looks like.

Charlie   And when I see her –

Moe   We get out and grab her.

Charlie   . . . do you not want to see the photo too?

Moe   No.

Beat.

Charlie   What about the name –

Moe   Don't tell me anything.

Charlie   . . . does that make it easier for you?

. . . if like, if you don't know names, or –

Moe   Who's doing the main job.

Charlie   . . .

Moe   Who?

Charlie   Y-you.

Moe   I am. I'm doing it. Why am I doing it?

Charlie   Because –

Moe   Because you can't. You couldn't.

. . .

Could you.

Never.

. . .

You'd just wait –

You'd just sit and wait for her to come get you.

Wait for your ending.

So you look after that bit of paper there, you look after that.

That's *your* job, alright?

Pause.

Charlie   Sorry.

Pause.

What shall we talk about?

Moe   Nothing.

Charlie   We can't just sit here in silence –

Moe   Yes we can.

Charlie   But we should –

Moe   *Yes* we can.

Pause.

Charlie   Do you think she was bluffing?

Pause.

You don't believe her.

About The Girl?

. . .

She was just saying that so we'd –

. . .

. . .

She doesn't exist, does she.

She's like a myth.

Moe   . . .

. . .

I don't know.

Pause.

Charlie   Do you know what they say about her?

Moe   . . .

Charlie   They say if you see her, it's like seeing death.

No one who ever meets her stays alive.

. . .

Except, you know.

The people she works for.

Everyone else who ever met her is dead now.

. . .

And she doesn't even do the killing, she's just like the, the *judge*.

She just decides.

But she decides, like, *how* it happens.

. . .

You know?

Moe   Don't think about it.

Charlie   I can't not think about it –

Moe   If we do the job, we don't have to worry about it.

Charlie   The job is still – It's still – *Murder*, or –

Moe   She did something.

To have this happen.

. . .

There are *reasons*.

Charlie *nods.*

Pause.

Charlie   I – Um –

Appreciate.

What you're doing –

For me.

Moe   I'm not doing anything for you.

Charlie   No, but –

If you didn't do . . .

This thing.

Like you said.

I couldn't . . .

We'd be dead.

. . .

You know, I'm pretty good at not thinking about things, but, this is, this is a hard . . .

I'm having a hard time not thinking about this.

. . .

Moe   What are you doing here?

Charlie   . . . what?

Moe   What are you doing in this car with me? Why are you here?

Charlie   It's my job –

Moe   Why don't you work in a shop or something? A normal job.

Charlie   I'm good at my job –

Moe   Your job is standing with me on an empty plot of land.

Charlie   We have to, to, stop people coming in, and wave the vans in –

Moe   What's in the vans?

Beat.

What's in them? What are you guarding?

What is your job?

Charlie   Security –

Moe   Security for what?

Charlie   Just like – Stolen goods or something.

Moe   That's what you think?

Charlie   That's what I sort of, *tell* myself. Or like counterfeit, counterfeit –

Moe   That's what they're driving in and taking underground.

Charlie   Yeah.

Moe   They need to keep fake jeans underground.

Charlie   Maybe –

Moe   That's what you tell people.

Charlie   I don't –

Moe   Your friends, your –

Charlie   I don't have any friends.

Moe   Whoever the fuck – Whoever you tell. You tell them –

Charlie   I have two friends.

Moe   You tell them you're a security guard.

Charlie   Yes.

Moe   And you just tell yourself it's nothing – You just don't think about it.

Charlie   No –

Moe   And now we're going to do this, and you're just going to not think about this too.

Pause.

Charlie   I –

Moe   This is real. All of this.

Charlie   I know –

Moe   So why are you involved?

Charlie   I'm not involved, I just work –

Moe   *Why.*

Charlie   Because. Because I couldn't get any other job.

. . .

Beat.

Moe   No other job.

Charlie   No.

Moe   No other job would take you.

Charlie   No.

Moe   You can't get a job stacking shelves or –

Charlie   No I can't. I tried already.

Moe   For how long?

Charlie   I thought you didn't want to talk.

Moe   You don't like talking now I'm asking *you* the questions.

Charlie   I can't get a job because I have a, a *record*.

. . .

Okay?

Beat.

Moe   A record.

Charlie *nods.*

Moe   A jail –

Charlie *nods.*

Moe   You've been in jail.

Charlie   A sort of a – Yeah. Yes.

Pause.

Moe   Bollocks.

Charlie   I did.

Moe   Bollocks.

Charlie   I did as well.

Beat.

Moe   For what.

Charlie   . . .

Moe   What did you do?

Charlie   Nothing –

Moe   You didn't do anything.

Charlie   No.

Moe   People don't go to jail for –

Charlie   Well I did.

Pause.

My friend. At school.

. . .

My friend took a gun to school.

. . .

Pause.

Moe   A gun.

Charlie *nods.*

Moe   And he killed someone.

Charlie   . . . two people.

Pause.

Moe   And you helped.

Charlie   No I didn't help. Course I didn't help –

Moe   Well you're helping now –

Charlie   I didn't *help*.

Moe   Then what?

Charlie   I was just there.

. . .

By accident.

. . .

He told me to follow him.

. . .

Then he went in their – Their form –

And he took this gun out his pocket.

Like an old, an old gun –

. . .

And he shot them.

. . .

And cos I was there . . .

They thought I was –

We planned it or something.

. . .

I had this notebook that I wrote in.

And it had a lot of angry stuff in there.

I used to be really angry.

So they thought –

You know.

Pause.

Moe   No one will give you a job, because it says on your –

Charlie   You have to declare it.

Beat.

Moe   So then some guy – You hear –

Charlie   Gale.

Moe   Gale finds you somewhere –

And she puts you with me.

Charlie   . . . I'm in charge of the mobile.

. . .

I have to run and hide and call her.

If we see something.

. . .

That's my job.

Pause.

Moe   Play your game.

Charlie   Don't want to.

Moe   It's fine.

Charlie   I don't want to.

Moe   . . .

Pause.

Charlie   What do you think they do.

Moe   What.

Charlie   What's in the vans. What goes underground.

Moe   . . .

Charlie   Do you know?

Moe   No I don't know.

Charlie   But you have a theory.

Moe   No . . .

Charlie   You have an opinion.

Moe   . . .

Charlie   What is it?

Pause.

Moe   Do you know what a snuff film is?

Pause.

They sit in silence.

/ eleven.

Fay *and* **Gale**.

Fay *is clutching a laptop.*

Gale   What are you doing in here.

Pause.

You're not to come in here.

Fay   Where is she.

Gale   This is my office, you can't come in here.

Did you hear me?

Fay   Where *is* she.

Gale   Where's *who*?

Who are we talking about?

. . .

Your little friend?

Your buddy?

Fay   . . .

Gale   She's gone.

She left.

Fay   She left.

Gale   She left.

Fay   Like the others.

Gale   It's not a long-term job. People leave.

Why do you have my laptop?

Fay   What happened to her.

Gale   I *told* you –

Fay   All of them. Three now. All just left.

Gale   She came to me –

Fay   She *came* to you –

Gale   She came to me and explained she was leaving.

Fay   Overnight.

Gale   Yes overnight. She left.

Fay   Where.

Gale   I'm not her keeper.

. . .

Put it down.

. . .

She *left*.

I don't know where.

Just because you haven't the strength to leave yourself –

Fay   They didn't leave –

Gale   Just because you've *nailed* yourself to that bed, doesn't mean others –

Fay   They didn't *leave*. They're *gone*.

Gale   People move on. This is what happens. When you save enough money to leave, you leave.

. . .

Put it *down*.

Pause.

Fay   I broke in here.

Gale   I can see. I see this.

Fay   I broke the door to get in here.

Gale   And now you're fired. Can you understand that? You're fired.

You don't even have this any more. You don't even –

Fay   Why do you have our blood types.

Pause.

On your laptop –

Gale   That is my / personal –

Fay   On your *laptop*. You have a list of everyone's blood type. All of us.

Everyone who ever worked here.

People who left – Who I *thought* had left, maybe you took them too –

Gale   I don't *take* anyone –

Fay   *All* of us.

. . .

Why do you have this?

How do you even *get* this –

Gale   Put it down.

Fay   What's happening here.

Gale   Put it back on my desk and walk –

Fay   Where are they?

Gale   You –

She steps forward –

Fay   Stop. *Stand*. I'll scream –

Gale   Listen –

Fay   I'll scream and bring everyone running in here

Stand there. Still. Don't *fucking* move!

Pause.

What's happening.

Gale   Nothing is happening –

Fay   *Fuck* you.

. . .

I can *feel* it. I can literally *feel* it. Right now. All around us.

All around *this*.

This is something –

Gale   Why do you care?

Fay   You –

Gale   Why are you getting involved?

. . .

Why do you put yourself in these situations?

Over and over.

Pain and misery, pain and misery, again and again, again and again.

You climb out of one hole and dig yourself another.

As if you *want* it.

As if you *crave* it.

. . .

And now you're going to get involved in this?

Over *her*?

Over some drifter who'd do anything if you waved enough money at her?

. . .

Did she tell you the kind of films she was making?

. . .

Put it down, walk away, forget about it.

Pause.

Fay   Sit.

Sit down.

Beat.

Gale *sits.*

Pause.

Fay   I'm leaving here with this.

Gale   Listen –

Fay   Shut up. Stop talking.

I'm leaving with this.

I'm taking it to the police, to, to, to everyone –

I'm going to show this to everyone.

Do you understand?

. . .

They'll come here –

Gale   You're going to go to the police.

Fay   Yes.

Gale   You, with everything –

Fay   Yes.

Gale   Everything that happened to you.

. . .

Straight to the police.

. . .

Straight back to him.

. . .

I wouldn't recommend it.

Fay   I don't care –

Gale   I wouldn't recommend it.

Fay   *Shut* up.

Pause.

Gale   If you leave here, with that.

If you call the police, if you don't call the police –

There are people who will come looking for you.

. . .

Okay?

There are people who will want to know who you are, and what you look like, and I'll have to tell, I'll have to tell them.

Okay?

They'll come looking for you.

And they'll find you.

These people –

They find everybody.

Doesn't matter about police.

Doesn't matter how far you run.

How fast.

Where you go.

They find *everybody*.

Do you understand?

. . .

Do you hear me?

. . .

Do you *hear* me?

/ twelve.

Keaton *and* **Charlie**.

Keaton *rolls dice.*

Charlie   Success! The door swings open and you flee from the sacrificial chamber clutching the Necronomicon book to your chest.

Keaton   Which way do I go?

Charlie   The hall splits into two, will you go left or right?

Keaton   Uh – Uh – Left – No, Right!

Charlie *rolls dice.*

Charlie   As you run down the hall you collide with the High Priest of the Cthulhu Cult –

Keaton   No!

Charlie (*in character*)   You miserable worm, you thought you stood a chance against the might of the Old Ones?

Keaton   What you're doing is wrong –

Charlie   Wrong? Such a ludicrously *human* concept. The universe cares not for *wrong*, girl. And soon, neither shall *you* –

He pulls a rusty hook from his robes –

Keaton   Uh – Uh –

Charlie   (Remember you've still got the revolver.)

Keaton   Uh – Duck between his legs and run past him!

Charlie   Duck between –

Keaton *and* **Charlie** *roll dice.*

Charlie   Wow! You duck between his legs and run; after a moment of confusion he dashes after you, waving his hook –

It's too late, girl!

Keaton   Run!

Charlie   The dawning of the new age shall make slaves of you all!

The walls and floor around you start rumbling –

Keaton   Run!

Charlie   He is risen! Prepare the fruits of your body for sacrifice!

Keaton   *Run!*

Charlie   The stone starts crumbling, the walls are falling around you, you hear an unholy noise and turn to see –

Keaton   What?

Charlie   *Wait!*

. . .

I need a wee. Wee break.

He dashes off.

Keaton *sits.*

She is perfectly still and silent.

Time passes.

Charlie *comes back in with lemonade.*

Charlie   I brought lemonade. I'm thirsty. Are you thirsty?

Keaton   Okay.

He pours it.

Charlie   It's like proper stuff, it's yellow, see? Old-fashioned.

They drink.

Pause.

You're playing really well, but you could definitely afford to use your weapons more.

Keaton   I don't want to.

Charlie   That's what they're there for –

Keaton   I don't like to.

Charlie   Okay.

Well that's the great thing about RPGs, there's no limit on the ways to play.

They drink.

Pause.

Do you think you want to do something else another time?

Keaton   What.

Charlie   Do you want to go to the cinema one time?

Keaton   . . .

Charlie   We can go watch a film or something. If you want.

Keaton   . . . why.

Charlie   Why?

. . .

Cos – We're friends.

Keaton   Oh.

. . .

I can't.

She drinks.

Charlie   Oh, okay.

He drinks.

Pause.

Charlie   I can't play for much longer. I have to go to work.

Keaton   Why.

Charlie   Because, it's my job. I'm a security guard, I told you.

Keaton   What are you a security guard for.

Charlie   Like, *why* am I a security guard, or, like, *what* do I keep secure?

Keaton   What are you guarding.

Charlie   It's kind of –

I actually don't know –

Keaton   Why.

Charlie   It's a secret.

Keaton   Why.

Charlie   Because – Uh – I don't know if it's, um, *legal*, or not.

Keaton   Why.

Charlie   You talk weird.

Keaton   . . . I do?

Charlie   Yeah.

Keaton   . . . why is it illegal?

Charlie   I don't *know* it's illegal, I just – They don't tell me what it is, so maybe it's *not* legal.

. . .

Do you know where Pomona is?

Beat.

Keaton   . . . what.

Charlie   It's like this weird place in town, like, right in the centre. It's like an island? I think it used to be a dock, but now there's nothing on it, it's just this bit of land with the canal on either side, and it's all full of crumbly cement and weeds and stuff.

No one goes there, it's sort of like a forgotten place.

That's where I work.

It's kind of creepy at night because there's no street lights, so it's just pitch-black there –

Keaton   Why do you work there.

Charlie   Because. I do. It's weird, I know –

Keaton   Why do you have to guard it.

Charlie   I don't guard the whole of it – There's just only one road that goes in and out, and me and my friend we have to stand there and stop people going in, cos it's like, private, you know, and then, most days this van shows up, and we have to unlock the gate and let it in.

It's a very easy job.

Boring though sometimes.

He drinks.

All the vans that drive in, they drive right to the middle, cos there's this hatch there, that leads underground?

And there's these tunnels that used to have all cables or something to do with the old dock stuff, but they're just tunnels now, and apparently if you follow them they lead to like these huge old air-aid shelters. Like these sort of massive caves they dug in the war.

I never saw them, but that's what they say's down there.

And I heard now they have power down there and everything, like it's this big warehouse down there, all done up –

Keaton   You shouldn't work there.

Charlie   What – Why?

Keaton   . . .

Charlie   I don't ever go down there, I just let the vans –

Keaton   I don't want to talk about it. I want to play again.

Pause.

Charlie   What's wrong?

Beat.

Keaton   I want to play.

Pause.

Stop talking and play the game again.

Charlie   Okay – Hang on – Uh –

So –

Keaton   I'm running.

Charlie   Yeah, you're running, but the stone is all crumbling, the walls are falling around you, and then you hear an unholy noise and turn to see –

Hold on –

He fumbles in a bag and pulls on a Cthulhu mask.

Charlie   The mighty, horrific form of Cthulhu rising up from the ground and destroying the castle behind you –

Evil has awoken! The Dark Lord has risen to reclaim what is his!

Keaton*'s phone beeps.*

She looks at it.

Beat.

Keaton   I have to go.

Charlie   Oh –

Keaton   I have to go now.

Charlie   Well maybe tomorrow –

She's gone.

Bye.

/ thirteen.

Fay *and* **Moe**.

Fay   The shower's just in there, there's towels in there.

Moe   Oh –

Fay   Just shower up and we can start.

Moe   I don't want a shower.

Fay   Afraid you need to have a shower.

Moe   I don't – I mean –

Fay   Afraid I insist on showers.

Moe   I don't want to have any – What you think I want.
I don't want that.

Fay   What's that?

Moe   S-sex. I don't want sex.

Beat.

Moe   Sorry.

Fay   You'd like a massage.

Moe   N-no. No.

Fay   So what do you want.

Beat.

Moe   I'd just like to –

. . .

Can we just sit. And talk.

For a while.

Beat.

Fay   Okay.

They sit.

Moe *sits as far away as he can.*

Pause.

Fay   You just want to sit like this?

Moe   For a bit.

Fay   And talk.

Moe Yes.

Fay Talk about –

Moe About anything.

Fay . . .

Moe . . .

Fay Well it's up to you –

Moe Do you have a family?

Fay I'm not talking about that.

Moe Why not?

Fay Because I'm not talking about personal – Personal things.

Moe What if I pay you more?

Fay You can't *buy* conversation.

Moe It's not, it's just –

Fay I'd drop it. I'd drop this.

Moe Sorry.

. . .

Is this a good place to work?

Fay No.

Moe It's not.

Fay Of course it's not.

Moe Why not?

Fay Because I have to have sex with people for money.

Moe (*nods*) Right. Yeah.

Pause.

Fay What do you want?

Moe I –

Fay   If it's weird, just ask. I'll only say no.

Moe   I'd just like to touch you.

Fay   Touch me.

Moe   Yes.

Fay   Just touch me.

Moe *nods.*

Fay   This is like – Your thing. This is what you like. To touch.

Moe   No –

Fay   It's fine.

Moe   No, it's not that. It's not a, a sex thing –

Fay   What then?

Pause.

Moe   . . . I have some –

Issues.

I have issues with, uh –

Violence.

. . .

. . .

I'm in groups. I'm in a lot of *groups*.

For my violence issues.

Beat.

Fay   We have a lot of security here –

Moe   No – I won't – I won't hurt you – / I have –

Fay   You can leave if you're thinking –

Moe   No – I'm not – I wouldn't. I'm just sitting all the way over here, it's not an issue, I won't –

I won't even come near you.

I'll sit here.

I'm all the way over here, so you don't have to . . .

. . .

I'm getting help for it.

I'm in groups. Like I said.

. . .

It's a lot of exercises.

And,

Positive thinking.

Things like that.

. . .

I used to be very . . .

But now –

I'm not –

I don't hurt people anymore.

. . .

Fay   So now you pay women to touch you.

Moe   No, I – Not to touch *me*, I –

Fay   What.

Moe   I can't touch people. Any more.

I don't –

I mean, I haven't touched anyone.

For a long time.

Because I was scared I'd –

. . .

I feel very disconnected.

Because I don't touch people.

I feel very,

Uh,

Disconnected.

Pause.

Fay   I don't feel sorry for you.

Moe   No – Definitely –

Fay   I have no sympathy.

Moe   No.

Pause.

Fay   Who did you hurt?

Moe   . . . a lot of people.

. . .

My family.

Fay   Your wife?

Moe (*nods*)   My ex-wife.

. . .

A lot of people.

My parents.

My brother.

Just people – On the street.

I got in fights with people on the street.

I'd just hit people on the street.

. . .

I put a lot of people in hospital.

I can't count how many.

Beat.

Fay   That's disgusting.

Moe   Yeah.

Fay   That's awful.

Moe   Yeah.

Pause.

Have you ever hurt anyone?

Fay   No.

Moe   Has anyone ever hurt you?

Pause.

Fay   . . . my husband.

Moe *nods.*

Fay   My husband hurt me.

And my daughter.

. . .

Can you understand that?

Moe   I can't . . . really –

Speak for anyone else.

I don't know him.

. . .

Do you think I'm like him?

Fay   . . . no.

You're quiet.

. . .

He hates women.

Moe *nods.*

Fay   Do you hate women?

Moe   No.

Fay   The whole world hates women.

Moe   Maybe. Not me. I don't think.

. . .

Are you safe now?

Fay   Never.

Never safe.

Moe *nods.*

Beat.

Fay   You think you're different.

Moe   I –

Fay   You think you're different from other men.

Don't you.

Moe   . . .

The people in my group – a lot of them –

They're like your –

Fay   My husband.

Moe   Yes.

Fay   But you're different.

Moe   I don't . . .

Beat.

Moe   . . .

I just want everything to stop.

Fay   You want to kill yourself.

Moe   No . . .

Fay   What then.

Moe   I want to . . . go to sleep.

And wake up.

And there's no one left.

Everyone's gone.

. . .

Then I could die.

Knowing it was all done.

I think that would be an amazing . . .

An amazing kind of peace.

Pause.

Fay *takes her shoe off.*

She very slowly stretches her leg across the gap between them.

Moe *reaches, tentatively.*

He stops breathing.

He holds her foot.

The world falls around them. \

/fourteen.

The lights die.

Ollie *is underground.*

She walks down a long tunnel with a flashlight, breathing hard.

/fifteen.

Gale *and* **Keaton**.

Silence.

Gale   She *has* –

Left.

With the, the lap – My laptop.

. . .

But –

I have two men . . .

I'll give them all the information.

I'll tell them.

They'll find her.

. . .

And she won't go far –

She has previous –

Her husband –

She won't go to the police.

If she can help it.

. . .

At least not immediately.

Not for a, a while.

. . .

And the men –

They're good. They'll find her.

I'll – I'll tell them to –

They'll get it done.

Pause.

Of course, now you know who she is, and –

If you wanted –

To just take her . . .

Yourself. You could take her yourself –

. . .

I mean.

It's my mess.

I'll clean it up.

Of course.

. . .

It'll –

It's not a problem.

I promise you.

I'll fix this.

Pause.

Gale   If you need to know anything else, maybe –

If there's anything else you *need* –

. . .

Otherwise –

Keaton   Do you know what happens to the girls you give them.

Pause.

Gale   I have an – An idea.

Pause.

I think maybe –

You – *They* –

I think they use them to make sn-snuff films.

. . .

Keaton *shakes her head.*

Gale   No, yes.

Pause.

Not, not that.

Then I think maybe –

I don't, I don't know.

. . .

Pause.

Gale   Is that –

Keaton   They do two things.

Pause.

Gale   I don't really need to –

Keaton   They take the people.

The ones you give them.

And others. From all over. Men and women.

And they take all the organs out and sell them.

Pause.

And maybe they'll do that to you.

If I tell them.

I'll tell them to, and I'll tell them not to put you to sleep like they do with the others.

You'll be awake when they take yours out.

Pause.

Can you guess the second thing.

Pause.

Gale *shakes her head.*

Keaton   They take the girls that you give them.

And some others.

And they tie them down.

And they put babies inside them.

And then when the baby's ready,

They take it out and sell it.

And then they do it again. And again. And again.

And they keep going for years until they can't any more.

And then they take their organs out.

So maybe I'll tell them to do that to you instead.

Because it's both.

I'll tell them to put a baby in you.

You look like you'd make the kind of baby they could sell easy.

They'll make a lot of babies with you and then after years
they'll cut you open while you're awake, and they'll take out
what's left.

Pause.

Would you like that.

Pause.

Now that I've told you, you know.

So you'll fix this now.

Gale   . . .

Keaton   Because if you don't fix this by tomorrow.

Then I'll come and see you again.

And I'll tell them.

And they'll come and take you.

And I'll tell them to keep you awake.

And you'll be awake for a long time.

Do you see.

/sixteen.

Charlie *and* **Moe** *under a bridge.*

Rain. Cars overhead.

Fay *kneels on the ground in front of them, hands bound, a rucksack zipped over her head.*

Pause.

Charlie   Do we do it now, or . . .

Pause.

How are you going to, to –

Do it.

Pause.

She said we had to get a laptop.

She didn't have one with her. I didn't see one –

She said that's important. It said on the note we *have* to get the laptop. If we mess this up, then –

. . .

We have to get the laptop.

Pause.

Where's the laptop?

. . .

Please?

Beat.

She can't answer with the bag –

I have to –

He goes to take the bag off.

Moe   Don't do that.

Charlie   But –

Moe   I'm fucking *telling* you. Leave it.

Leave it on.

Pause.

Charlie   But the bag –

The bag makes it worse –

. . .

I can see –

She's breathing and it's making the, the material move –

Moe   You want her looking at you?

Charlie   Well she is – She is looking –

We can't just tell ourselves she's *not* looking –

We can't just pretend we're not –

. . .

I don't think we should do this,

I don't think we should do this now.

. . .

I think we shouldn't – We should . . .

Beat.

Moe   What?

Charlie   Something, some other – Some different –

Moe   There's no other way.

She's involved.

Charlie   We don't know −

Moe   She's involved, we're involved. So we're here.

Charlie   We don't *know* that. We don't even know what it is −
What it is we're involved *in* −

Moe   Stop crying.

Charlie   . . .

Moe   Stop it.

Pause.

Charlie   I don't want to do this any more . . .

I can't do this job . . .

I can't pretend any more.

I can't just put my fingers in my ears −

We're not security guards. We're *not*.

I can't make myself believe that any more −

Moe   Calm down.

Charlie   I can't *do* this now.

I'm a good person.

I try to be −

I think I am −

I'm trying −

I *try* to be a good person.

But this isn't −

Moe   Stop.

Charlie   I keep thinking that everything will get better but it
doesn't, it just gets worse, it's always got worse, and if I do this
then it'll be even worse than that.

Pause.

Moe   She's involved. We're involved.

This is what happens.

Charlie   But –

Moe   If we don't do our job, then they'll find us in pieces in the canal. Okay? Remember?

She will come and find us.

Charlie   She's not real . . .

Moe   It's *all* real.

All of it.

Everything bad is real.

. . .

And this is where the roads meet. This is an inevitability.

. . .

And I don't care what happens to me.

But you're in this. You're involved.

Charlie   You don't care about me . . .

Moe   . . .

I wish I didn't.

Charlie   You don't.

You don't care about anything.

Moe   . . .

When I think about you getting killed over this,

I feel like that's, that's something I wish didn't happen.

. . .

I haven't felt like that about anything for a while.

. . .

Even if it is –

Charlie   You know her.

Beat.

When you saw her, you looked at her funny because you *know* her.

. . .

And you're still going to do it.

Moe   I don't –

Charlie   You're still going to do it even though you *know* her –

Moe   What does it *matter*?

What does it *matter* if I know her?

Would it make it better if I didn't?

. . .

What does *any* of it matter?

All of this.

All of it.

It's just a cycle of *shit*.

A drowning in oceans of piss.

I should be in jail. Or dead. Even better.

Why aren't I?

Why didn't anyone make that happen?

What kind of fucking world is this where *I'm* still allowed to walk around?

Why would I want to live in a world that would let me walk on it?

Why would anyone want to live somewhere like that?

. . .

But I believe in you. You're a good –

Charlie   I'm not –

Moe   You're a *good* person.

You're *trying* to be a good person.

. . .

And that's enough.

It's enough just to try.

He takes a knife from his pocket.

Moe   So if I have to do this to keep you above water, then that's –

That's okay –

Charlie *goes to take the bag off.*

Moe   Don't –

Don't *fucking touch her* –

The bag is off.

Fay, *gagged, looks at* **Moe**.

Pause.

She wobbles to her feet.

Pause.

She runs off.

Pause.

Charlie *wipes his face on his sleeve.*

Pause.

Moe   Hit me.

/seventeen.

Ollie *is deeper into the tunnels.*

Her flashlight illuminates **Charlie**.

Charlie   After following the tip from the man in the car, you head to Pomona and sneak past the two guards.

It is barren and empty and overgrown and you see and hear no one but cars passing in the distance.

You walk on cracked concrete until your foot steps on metal and you find a hatch hidden in amongst the tall grass.

Moe *and* **Gale** *roll dice.*

Charlie   You find yourself in a deep underground tunnel.

Looking around you, it seems to have originally housed cables, but is tall enough for you to stand up in. The water at your feet is brown with rust and dirt. Far ahead of you you see a dim light.

Ollie   Keep going.

Zeppo *and* **Keaton** *roll dice.*

Charlie   You press on until the light grows nearer, and you find yourself at a large, steel door. It looks newer than your surroundings, and is locked firmly.

Ollie   Um – Pick the lock –

Fay *and* **Charlie** *roll dice.*

Charlie   You fail.

Ollie   Look around the tunnel –

Moe *and* **Gale** *roll dice.*

Charlie   You find nothing of use.

Ollie   Uh –

Charlie   You hear voices on the other side of the door –

Ollie   Hide in the shadows –

All six roll dice.

Charlie   You press against the wall as the door opens and a tall man in a leather jacket comes out into the tunnel to smoke.

Zeppo *and* **Keaton** *roll dice.*

Charlie   He walks a way down the tunnel into the gloom –

Ollie   Head inside –

All six roll dice.

Charlie   You find yourself in a brightly lit hallway.

The floor beneath you is tiled and spotless. Strip lights buzz above you.

Fay *and* **Charlie** *roll dice.*

Charlie   There are two doors – one to your left, and one ahead of you.

Ollie   Straight ahead.

All six roll dice.

Charlie   The door opens into a long room with a tall ceiling. It seems to be a medical ward of some sort. It is white and sterile. The walls are lined with beds.

All six roll dice.

Charlie   In most of the beds lies a figure tied down with straps. None of them are moving.

Ollie   Look closer –

All six roll dice.

Charlie   You step closer to one of the beds and find a young man strapped down. He wears a hospital gown. A drip is attached to his arm. His head is covered with a thick white stocking. A tube runs through the fabric into his nose.

All six roll dice.

You look under the gown at his body. There are a number of long cuts sealed with stitches. Some are bleeding. A catheter runs down his leg.

All six roll dice.

The ward is filled with about a hundred beds, a man or woman is strapped to the majority of them. The other beds are empty.

All six roll dice.

There's another door at the end of the ward.

Ollie   Go – Go through the door.

All six roll dice.

Charlie   You step into another almost identical ward, with a similar amount of beds. This time the patients are all women.

All six roll dice.

Charlie   The women are all at varying stages of pregnancy. Some have stomachs swollen at full term, others appear to be in much earlier stages. All seem to be asleep or unconscious. All are wearing the white stockings over their heads.

–   You hear voices in the previous room –
–   There's a door ahead of you to another room –
–   The voices get closer –
–   Go through the door –

Ollie   No, wait –

–   You emerge into a hallway.
–   Two more doors.

Ollie   Go back –

–   You are looking for your sister –
–   You enter the left door.
–   Another white room
–   Another ward
–   Rows and rows of clear plastic cradles

- Some empty
- Some with child
- Babies here
- Arms and legs swimming in the air
- A voice at the end of the room shouts
- Move
- Quickly
- Get out of here
- Back out
- Into the hall
- One door left
- Looking for an exit
- You are looking for your sister
- The door is different
- Steel and heavy like the first
- Open
- Pull
- Into the room
- The last room
- And the heat overwhelms you
- Blinds you
- The smell invades your skull
- Makes you sway
- Drunk with the stench
- The furnace dominates the room
- The flames furious
- A second machine grinds
- Churning
- There are huge plastic tubs on wheels
- Filled with ash
- Grey gravelled
- Ash
- Filled
- Turn and leave
- Quickly
- You are looking for your sister
- They will find you

- Do not pass this point.
- You are looking for your sister –

All seven roll dice.

- You want to see the daylight again
- Back
- Back in the room

All seven roll dice.

- Back in the ward
- The ward with the women
- Voices in the next room
- You are looking for your sister –

All seven roll dice.

- Under the bed
- Hide under the bed
- Voices near
- You are looking
- Two men
- Are putting a new one
- A new patient
- The new patient
- You won't get out
- Strapping her to the bed
- On this bed
- Tied down
- Strapped down
- Her clothes fall around you
- Your heartbeat deafens
- can't breathe
- can't blink
- You won't get out of here alive
- You'd be
- Lucky
- You'd be lucky

All of them roll dice, again and again and again throughout the following.

- You'd be lucky to get
- You feel the hand close around your ankle
- You'd be lucky
- You feel the hand
- The hand
- The hand pulls
- The hand pulls you out into the open
- You'd be lucky to get out of here
- dead.

One last dice is rolled and they all lean in to see the number.

/eighteen.

Charlie *is flying high over the city.*

Charlie   Whoa –

He looks down at the sprawl beneath him.

Charlie   Am I dead?

Zeppo *is here. He's a seagull.*

Charlie   Hey. Hey – Excuse me –

Zeppo   What?

Charlie   Am I dead?

Zeppo   *What?*

Charlie   Am I dead? Am I like a ghost now?

Zeppo   I don't know. I don't know you.

I don't know if you're dead or not.

Pause.

Charlie   What kind of bird are you?

Zeppo   I'm a seagull.

Charlie   Am I a bird?

Zeppo   I don't know.

Charlie   . . . You're a seagull?

Zeppo   I told you.

Beat.

Charlie   How come you're here?

Zeppo   What?

Charlie   This isn't the sea – Aren't you supposed to be at the sea?

Zeppo   I can fly wherever I want.

Charlie   I just thought seagulls only stayed near the sea.

Zeppo   Well I don't care what you think. You're not in charge of me.

Beat.

Charlie   I was just asking.

Pause.

Zeppo   I'm working.

Charlie   You work here?

Zeppo   Yes.

Charlie   What's your job?

Zeppo   I'm trying to cover the whole city in shit.

Charlie   Wow.

Zeppo   Yeah.

Charlie   All of it?

Zeppo   Everything.

Charlie   The whole city?

Zeppo   Yes. I want to cover everyone and everything in my shit.

You won't be able to even tell it was a city ever,

Cos it'll just be covered in my shit.

Charlie   That's impressive. I have a similar plan, except with jizz.

Zeppo   With what?

Charlie   With my jizz. Semen.

Zeppo   . . .

That's weird. You're weird.

Pause.

Charlie   I never finished the game.

Zeppo   What game.

Charlie   My game I was playing with this girl.

Zeppo   There's always a girl.

Charlie   We were on a cliffhanger . . .

Zeppo   You should've killed her.

Charlie   What?

Zeppo   The person. You were supposed to kill. She'd have been better off.

You'd all be better off.

Beat.

Charlie   couldn't.

Zeppo   Why not.

Charlie   . . .

Zeppo   You were happy when your friend killed those two kids.

Weren't you?

Charlie   . . .

Zeppo   You didn't realise till afterwards.

But you were glad.

You're *still* glad.

You just wish you hadn't seen it.

Pause.

Charlie   Everyone looks so small.

Zeppo   They are small.

Charlie   . . .

Zeppo   They're nothing.

/nineteen.

Pomona.

Keaton *is here.*

Ollie *stumbles around aimlessly, cheerfully. She wears a hospital gown.*

Ollie   Hey.

Pause.

Hello.

Pause.

I just came out the ground over there.

Pause.

Do you recognise me?

Beat.

Keaton *shakes her head.*

Ollie   Oh.

. . .

I came out – There's a hatch – I came out the ground over there.

. . .

I woke up in a bed wearing this.

There were all wires coming out of me.

And I felt a hand on my leg and it pulled me out of my sleep and into the light.

I don't think I was supposed to wake up, but I did.

Pause.

Ollie   There's all people down there. In beds, like me.

And I saw a woman under a bed and they pulled her out of the bed and I was awake so I got up and left.

There's lots of people down there.

. . .

Shall I show you?

Keaton *shakes head.*

Beat.

Ollie   What's your name?

Keaton   . . . keaton.

Ollie   Keaton. Hello Keaton.

I don't know my name.

. . .

Are you okay?

Keaton   My friend is dead.

Ollie   Your friend is dead?

Keaton   I saw him over there. Under that bridge. He's dead.

Pause.

Ollie   I'm sorry.

. . .

I'm sorry about that.

Beat.

Keaton   I won't know how the story ends now.

Ollie   The story?

Keaton   We were playing a game. With a story. And he didn't get to the end.

Ollie   Oh.

. . .

I'm sorry about that.

Keaton   A great evil force awoke and I had to defeat it. But I won't know now.

Pause.

Ollie   Are you sad about your friend?

Keaton   . . .

What?

Ollie   Are you sad? About your friend being dead.

Pause.

Keaton   Yes.

. . .

I am.

. . .

Pause.

Ollie   I'm sad myself.

Keaton   Why.

Ollie   Because I've lost my sister.

Keaton   You have a sister.

Ollie   I think I do.

I think I have a sister and I think she came here somewhere and I think she's in trouble now.

. . .

I think she's in trouble.

. . .

Do you know how I can find her?

Pause.

Keaton   There's a road that goes all the way around the city.

Ollie   Yes.

Keaton   You have to go and stand on that road at night.

Ollie   Yes.

Keaton   A man drives round it every night in his car.

Ollie   Yes.

Keaton   Late at night.

Ollie   Yes.

Keaton   And the man knows everything about the city because he owns most of the city himself.

Ollie   Yes.

Keaton   If you ask him he might know how to help you.

Ollie   Yes.

. . .

The road around the city.

Pause.

It's very quiet here, that's for sure.

They stand and listen.

Cars on a busy road off in the distance.

Keaton   I should burn it all down.

Ollie   What?

Keaton   I should burn it all to nothing.

But they'd just start again.

. . .

Ollie *smiles at her.*

Pause.

Keaton *picks up a Rubik's Cube and starts solving it.*

Ollie *does the same.*

Soon, all seven characters are solving a cube each.

When they finish, they drop their cube and leave the stage.

One by one.

Ollie *is last.*

She tosses her solved cube to the floor.

She listens to the road.

Ollie   . . . It sure is quiet here . . .

She leaves the stage.

Exit.

Notes

The actor playing Ollie plays two characters.
In Scenes One, Seven, Fourteen and Seventeen she plays Ollie.
In Scenes Five, Nine and Nineteen she plays Ollie's twin sister.

The actors playing Ollie and Fay should not at any point be
wearing sexually suggestive or revealing clothing, despite their
employment.

DRAMA ONLINE

A new way to study drama

From curriculum classics
to contemporary writing
Accompanied by
theory and practice

Discover. Read. Study. Perform.

Find out more:
www.dramaonlinelibrary.com

 FOLLOW US ON TWITTER @DRAMAONLINELIB

Bloomsbury Methuen Drama Contemporary Dramatists

include

John Arden (two volumes)
Arden & D'Arcy
Peter Barnes (three volumes)
Sebastian Barry
Mike Bartlett
Dermot Bolger
Edward Bond (eight volumes)
Howard Brenton (two volumes)
Leo Butler
Richard Cameron
Jim Cartwright
Caryl Churchill (two volumes)
Complicite
Sarah Daniels (two volumes)
Nick Darke
David Edgar (three volumes)
David Eldridge (two volumes)
Ben Elton
Per Olov Enquist
Dario Fo (two volumes)
Michael Frayn (four volumes)
John Godber (four volumes)
Paul Godfrey
James Graham
David Greig
John Guare
Lee Hall (two volumes)
Katori Hall
Peter Handke
Jonathan Harvey (two volumes)
Iain Heggie
Israel Horovitz
Declan Hughes
Terry Johnson (three volumes)
Sarah Kane
Barrie Keeffe
Bernard-Marie Koltès (two volumes)
Franz Xaver Kroetz
Kwame Kwei-Armah
David Lan
Bryony Lavery
Deborah Levy
Doug Lucie

David Mamet (four volumes)
Patrick Marber
Martin McDonagh
Duncan McLean
David Mercer (two volumes)
Anthony Minghella (two volumes)
Tom Murphy (six volumes)
Phyllis Nagy
Anthony Neilson (two volumes)
Peter Nichol (two volumes)
Philip Osment
Gary Owen
Louise Page
Stewart Parker (two volumes)
Joe Penhall (two volumes)
Stephen Poliakoff (three volumes)
David Rabe (two volumes)
Mark Ravenhill (three volumes)
Christina Reid
Philip Ridley (two volumes)
Willy Russell
Eric-Emmanuel Schmitt
Ntozake Shange
Sam Shepard (two volumes)
Martin Sherman (two volumes)
Christopher Shinn
Joshua Sobel
Wole Soyinka (two volumes)
Simon Stephens (three volumes)
Shelagh Stephenson
David Storey (three volumes)
C. P. Taylor
Sue Townsend
Judy Upton
Michel Vinaver (two volumes)
Arnold Wesker (two volumes)
Peter Whelan
Michael Wilcox
Roy Williams (four volumes)
David Williamson
Snoo Wilson (two volumes)
David Wood (two volumes)
Victoria Wood

Bloomsbury Methuen Drama Modern Plays

include work by

Bola Agbaje
Edward Albee
Davey Anderson
Jean Anouilh
John Arden
Peter Barnes
Sebastian Barry
Alistair Beaton
Brendan Behan
Edward Bond
William Boyd
Bertolt Brecht
Howard Brenton
Amelia Bullmore
Anthony Burgess
Leo Butler
Jim Cartwright
Lolita Chakrabarti
Caryl Churchill
Lucinda Coxon
Curious Directive
Nick Darke
Shelagh Delaney
Ishy Din
Claire Dowie
David Edgar
David Eldridge
Dario Fo
Michael Frayn
John Godber
Paul Godfrey
James Graham
David Greig
John Guare
Mark Haddon
Peter Handke
David Harrower
Jonathan Harvey
Iain Heggie

Robert Holman
Caroline Horton
Terry Johnson
Sarah Kane
Barrie Keeffe
Doug Lucie
Anders Lustgarten
David Mamet
Patrick Marber
Martin McDonagh
Arthur Miller
D. C. Moore
Tom Murphy
Phyllis Nagy
Anthony Neilson
Peter Nichols
Joe Orton
Joe Penhall
Luigi Pirandello
Stephen Poliakoff
Lucy Prebble
Peter Quilter
Mark Ravenhill
Philip Ridley
Willy Russell
Jean-Paul Sartre
Sam Shepard
Martin Sherman
Wole Soyinka
Simon Stephens
Peter Straughan
Kate Tempest
Theatre Workshop
Judy Upton
Timberlake Wertenbaker
Roy Williams
Snoo Wilson
Frances Ya-Chu Cowhig
Benjamin Zephaniah

For a complete listing of Bloomsbury
Methuen Drama titles, visit:

www.bloomsbury.com/drama

Follow us on Twitter and keep up to date
with our news and publications

@MethuenDrama

9 781350 007420